BLOOMSBURY
PAST

First published 1993
by Historical Publications Ltd
32 Ellington Street, London N7 8PL
(Tel: 071-607 1628)

ISBN 0 948667 20 6

Typeset by Historical Publications Ltd
and Fakenham Photosetting

Printed by
Butler and Tanner,
Frome, Somerset.

BLOOMSBURY PAST

A Visual History

by
Richard Tames

HISTORICAL PUBLICATIONS

Acknowledgements

Special thanks are due to Richard Knight of the London Borough of Camden Local Studies Library and Archives, and to the staff of the Guildhall Library, the Paul Mellon Centre, and of Westminster Public Library.

The Illustrations

The following have kindly given their permission to reproduce illustrations:
The London Borough of Camden: 13, 15, 16, 17, 54, 55, 56, 68, 70, 74, 81, 87, 89, 107, 162, 171, 172, 173, 177, 181, 184, 186, 202, 203, 206, 211, 212, 217, 218
Coram Fields Children's Playground: 29
Guildhall Library, City of London: 31
National Portrait Gallery: 36, 134, 135, 145
Dr Williams' Library: 69
Slade School Archive: 119
Images, Lichfield WS13 6AA: 157
James Smith and Sons (Umbrellas) Ltd: 176, 178
Musée d'Art Moderne, Paris: 195
Andrew Nurnberg and Nicky Roberts: 215

All other illustrations were supplied by the Author, Roger Cline or Historical Publications Ltd

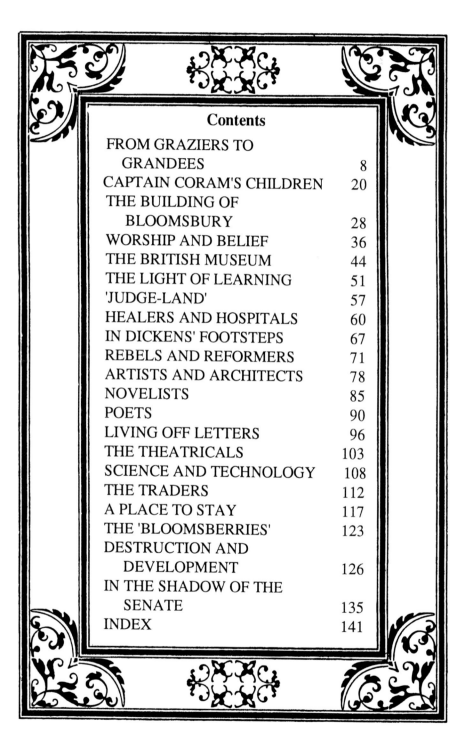

Contents

Further Reading

Borough of Holborn, Official Guide (1955).

Camden History Review, Vols 1, 2, 4, 6-9, 12, 14-16.

E. Beresford Chancellor, *London's Old Latin Quarter* (1930).

Catherine M. Clark and James M. Mackintosh, *London School of Hygiene and Tropical Medicine, Memoir 9*, 'The School and the Site' (1954).

George Clinch, *Bloomsbury and St Giles: Past and Present* (1890).

E.J. Davis, 'The University Site' in *London Topographical Record* Vol XVII (1936).

Peter Gibson, *The Capital Companion* (1985).

Edward Gordon and A.F.L. Deeson, *The Book of Bloomsbury* (1950).

Godfrey Heathcote Hamilton, *Queen Square* (1926).

Heal Collection, Camden Local Studies Library and Archive.

Robert Hewison, *Under Siege: Literary Life in London 1939-45* (1988).

Malcolm J. Holmes and Richard G. Knight, *Camden Past and Present: A Guide to Camden's Archives and Local Studies Collections* (London Borough of Camden 1989)

John Lehmann, *Holborn: An Historical Portrait of a London Borough* (1970).

R.H. Nichols and F.A. Wray, *The History of the Foundling Hospital* (1935)

Philip Norman, 'Queen Square, Bloomsbury and its Neighbourhood', in *London Topographical Record*, Vol. X (1916)

Donald J. Olsen, *The Growth of Victorian London* (1979)

Donald J. Olsen, *Town Planning in London: The Eighteenth and Nineteenth Centuries* (2nd edition 1982)

Alan and Veronica Palmer, *Who's Who in Bloomsbury* (1987)

S.P. Rosenbaum (ed.), *The Bloomsbury Group. A Collection of Memoirs, Commentary and Criticism* (University of Toronto Press 1975).

Sir John Summerson, *Georgian London* (rev. ed. 1962).

Survey of London, Vol. XXI, Tottenham Court Road and Neighbourhood (1949).

Survey of London, Vol. XXIV, King's Cross Neighbourhood (1952).

Gladys Scott Thomson, *The Russells in Bloomsbury 1669-1771* (1940).

Katherine Sturtevant, *Our Sisters' London: Nineteen Feminist Walks* (The Women's Press 1991).

Edward Walford, *Old and New London* (6 vols 1872-8).

Ben Weinreb and Christopher Hibbert, *The London Encyclopedia* (1983).

Introduction

'I find Bloomsbury fierce and scornful and stony-hearted, but... so adorably lovely that I look out of my window all day long.'

It is appropriate that a book about Bloomsbury should be prefaced by a quotation from Virginia Woolf; but one of the main purposes of this book is to illustrate how much more there is to Bloomsbury than the so-called Bloomsbury Group. Their cultured sensitivities stand in sharp contrast to the darker side of Bloomsbury's history, which is represented by duels and dog-fights, slums and scandals, brothels and riots.

Just as there is no definitive agreement about who was a member of the Bloomsbury Group, so there is no strict and unchallengeable definition of the area's borders. For the purposes of this book it is taken to be bounded on the west by Tottenham Court Road, on the north by Euston Road, to the east by Gray's Inn Road and to the south by New Oxford Street and Theobald's Road.

This is inevitably a book which is as much about people as places but it gives due credit to Bloomsbury's accomplished builders as well as to its talented residents. Even today the area's somewhat disfigured elegance represents what the urban historian Donald Olsen has hailed as one of the most significant and successful attempts at town planning in the entire history of the capital. Bloomsbury boasts not only London's oldest true square, but also its least altered square and its second largest one. And in his magisterial *'Georgian London'* Sir John Summerson placed particular emphasis on the significance of Bloomsbury in pioneering the building lease system through which half of the rest of the city has subsequently been built. Much of its architecture is anonymous in a positive sense - discreet and unpretentious; but its buildings include work by Hawksmoor, Nash, Smirke, Wilkins, Cubitt, Waterhouse, Baker, Holden and Lasdun, not to mention the capital's largest neo-Gothic church and the first to be built in the full-blooded style of the 'Greek Revival'.

Bloomsbury has had other firsts as well - the first London by-pass, the first public demonstration of a railway locomotive, the first experiment to calculate the weight of the earth, the first English feminist tract and magazine, the first British university to grant women degrees on the same terms as men and the first true museum in the modern sense of the word. Bloomsbury has been the birthplace of Faraday, Ruskin, Cruikshank, Trollope, Disraeli, William de Morgan and Samuel Coleridge-Taylor. In another sense it has been the birthplace of *Bleak House*, *The Waste Land* , *To the Lighthouse* and *The Haywain*.

If Oxford was the legendary home of lost causes Bloomsbury has been the natural nursery of progressive ones from penal reform, adult education and Christian Socialism to the Arts and Crafts movement, avant-garde aesthetics and feminism. Pre-eminently the home of idealists and intellectuals, of painters and of poets, Bloomsbury has also had its share of cranks and con-men; they, too, find a place in the following pages.

1. *An adaptation of the 'Agas' view of Holborn (c1560), showing the southern part of Bloomsbury and the original Southampton House*

From Graziers to Grandees

BLEMONDSBURY

Bloomsbury takes its name from the Blemond family, who held land in the area in the thirteenth century. It has been ingeniously suggested that Blemond (variously spelled Blemunt, Blemont etc.) is in fact a French translation of Cornhill, the name of an illustrious London family into which the Blemonds had married. The alternative, and more remote, possibility is that they ultimately hailed from an obscure hamlet called Blemont in Calvados.

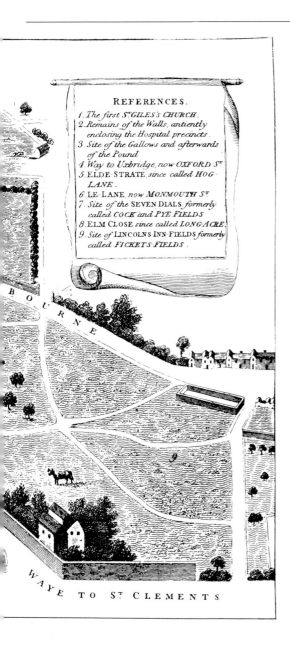

REFERENCES.

1. *The first St GILES's CHURCH.*
2. *Remains of the Walls, anciently enclosing the Hospital precincts.*
3. *Site of the Gallows and afterwards of the Pound.*
4. *Way to Uxbridge, now OXFORD St.*
5. *ELDE STRATE, since called HOG-LANE.*
6. *LE-LANE, now MONMOUTH St.*
7. *Site of the SEVEN DIALS, formerly called COCK and PYE FIELDS.*
8. *ELM CLOSE, since called LONG-ACRE.*
9. *Site of LINCOLNS INN-FIELDS, formerly called FICKETS-FIELDS.*

BOURNE

WAYE TO St CLEMENTS

The Blemonds' manor house ('bury') stood on some part of what is now Bloomsbury Square, almost certainly on the southern side. In the eleventh century the land had been an outlying farm belonging to Westminster Abbey; it is mentioned in the Domesday Book and in 1201 was sold by one John Bocointe to William Blemond, whose family forfeited it after the baronial revolt against Henry III in the 1260s.

Nevertheless the area was still referred to in 1281 as 'Blemundsberi" and the name remained with it henceforth. Its various owners over the next century were courtiers or leading citizens of London. Those who lived mainly in the provinces may have used the manor as a town house on their visits to the capital, while those who lived in London may have used it as an occasional country retreat. In either case they probably regarded it primarily as an investment, rather than a home, to be occupied and maintained by humbler tenants. In 1375 the area came into the possession of the Charterhouse, the great Carthusian monastery at Smithfield, which leased it out to tenants.

THE WRIOTHESLEYS

At the Dissolution Bloomsbury was seized by the Crown and in 1545 Henry VIII assigned it to his Lord Chancellor, Thomas Wriothesley. Wriothesley adroitly survived the death of his royal patron and was created Earl of Southampton in 1547, the year of Edward VI's accession. His descendant, Henry, the third Earl (Shakespeare's patron) ill-advisedly took part in the Earl of Essex's abortive rising of 1601, an escapade which was punished by the forfeiture of all his estates, including Bloomsbury. The separation was but brief. James I restored his lands and later tacked on a small area to the south thus giving the Bloomsbury estate a valuable Holborn frontage.

The fourth Earl of Southampton sided with Charles I in his quarrel with Parliament, a loyalty which cost him dear at the time but was ultimately well rewarded. In 1640 he obtained a royal licence to rebuild his residence on his Bloomsbury estate but the outbreak of the Civil War in 1642 put an abrupt halt to such peaceful pursuits as the Earl left London to rally to his king. A year later his Bloomsbury estate was the setting for a very different construction project as Parliament ringed the capital with a circuit of trenches, palisades and forts, hastily constructed of earth and timber. This defensive line (see Illustration 2) ran right through Bloomsbury, which was then on London's northern edge. Where houses now stand on the south side of Russell Square Parliament ordered the building of 'two batteries and a breastwork'; each battery, consisting of 'four brass demi-culverins', was protected by a double ditch and iron-tipped, yard-high stakes. The fortifications were allowed to decay after the emergency passed but the two bulwarks and their linking bank of earth were later skilfully incorporated as a terrace walk in the gardens of the future Bedford House and were not finally erased until the construction of Russell Square itself after 1800.

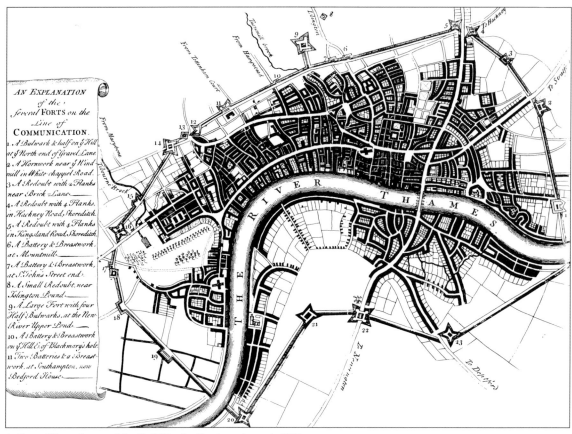

AN EXPLANATION
of the
several FORTS on the
Line of
COMMUNICATION.

1. A Bulwark & half on ye Hill at ye North end of Gravel Lane
2. A Hornwork near ye Wind mill in White chappel Road.
3. A Redoubt with 2 Flanks near Brick Lane.
4. A Redoubt with 4 Flanks in Hackney Road, Shoreditch.
5. A Redoubt with 4 Flanks in Kingsland Road, Shoreditch.
6. A Battery & Breastwork at Mountmill.
7. A Battery & Breastwork, at St Johns Street end.
8. A Small Redoubt, near Islington Pound.
9. A Large Fort with four Half-Bulwarks, at the New River Upper Pond.
10. A Battery & Breastwork on ye Hill E. of Blackmary's hole.
11. Two Batteries & a Breast-work, at Southampton, now Bedford House.

2. *Part of Vertue's map of the Civil War fortifications, drawn in 1738.*

THE LITTLE TOWN

Not until 1657 was the fourth Earl able to recommence the ambitious scheme for which the construction of his own palatial mansion would provide but a nucleus. The area in front of it would become what is now Bloomsbury Square and, discreetly tucked away nearby, there would be established a market to serve the needs of the square's inhabitants. Although Inigo Jones had developed Covent Garden as London's first continental-style piazza back in the 1620s, Bloomsbury Square was the first London square actually to be called a square, its first name being Southampton Square.

The scheme was dominated by the new Southampton House, built on the north side. Diarist Samuel Pepys refers to the project in October 1664 as 'a very great and noble work'. It consisted of a central block of three stories, flanked by wings of two stories. The first floor of the main block had eighteen principal rooms, with a further twenty-four rooms in the attic storey above and the ground floor and wings accounted for a further thirty-two rooms. The house and its gardens were surrounded with a brick wall with wrought iron gates.

Pepys's friend John Evelyn, who fancied himself as something of a connoisseur, made a visit in February 1665 and loftily recorded his verdict on what was by now 'a noble Square or Piazza, a little Town.' The Earl's house itself did not overly impress him - 'too low' - and its garden was still 'naked'; but he did concede that it had 'some noble rooms' and 'a pretty cedar chapel' and 'good air'.

To Dr. Everard Maynwaringe Bloomsbury's 'good air' was much more than a matter of passing remark. His *Treatise of the Scurvy*, published in the same year as Evelyn's visit, was lavish in its praises:

'.... I cannot but take notice of Bloomsbury for the best part about London, both for health and pleasure exceeding other places. It is the best air and finest prospect, being the highest ground, and overlooking other parts of the city. The fields bordering upon this place are very pleasant and dry grounds for walking and improving of health. A fit place for nobility and gentry to reside in that make their abode about London, there being the country air, pleasure and city conveniences joined together; now lately im-

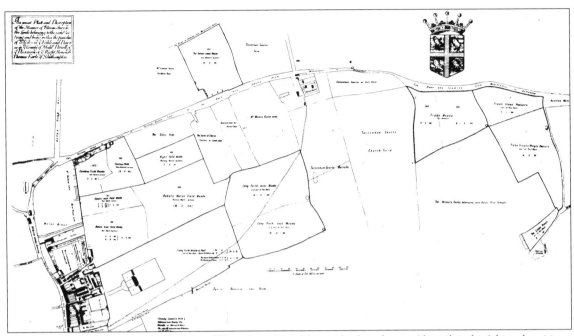

3. *A plan of the Earl of Southampton's manor of Bloomsbury, 1657. The map has been drawn with north to the right, and west to the top. Today's Oxford Street is the road to the top left of the plan, connecting with St Giles High Street. The residential quarter shown to the left of the plan is now bisected by New Oxford Street. The embryonic Great Russell Street can be seen running east-west to the right of the built-up area, with Southampton House set back from it.*

proved and built upon, and still increasing with fair and well contrived buildings, a good addition and ornament to this place.'

By now 'the void space in front of my lord's mansion' was being surrounded with new houses with frontages which varied from 24 feet to over sixty and whose tenants included a lord, a knight and a doctor. These prestigious residents soon found themselves joined by new neighbours as the Great Fire of 1666 drove thousands of the better-off from their accustomed homes in the City to seek healthy, fireproof, brick-built residences to the west. Bloomsbury might have been designed for the very purpose of their reception. By 1668 there were no less than 146 lessees on the estate and by 1683 there were to be more than fifty residences along Great Russell Street alone.

THE RUSSELLS IN BLOOMSBURY

The fourth Earl of Southampton died in May 1667, leaving three daughters but no son. His inheritance was divided between them by casting lots. The second daughter, Lady Rachel, was already the widow of Francis, Lord Vaughan, when she married William Russell, eldest surviving son of the Earl of Bedford in 1669 and as part of the marriage settlement she brought with her the Bloomsbury estate. Lady Rachel (1636-1723), ruled her grand house for over forty

4. *Thomas Wriothesley, 4th Earl of Southampton - a legacy by lots.*

5. Southampton (Bedford) House, which stood on the north side of Bloomsbury Square.

6. Bloomsbury Square in 1754, with Southampton (Bedford) House as its set-piece attraction; the hills of Hampstead and Highgate are in the distance. By Sutton Nicholls.

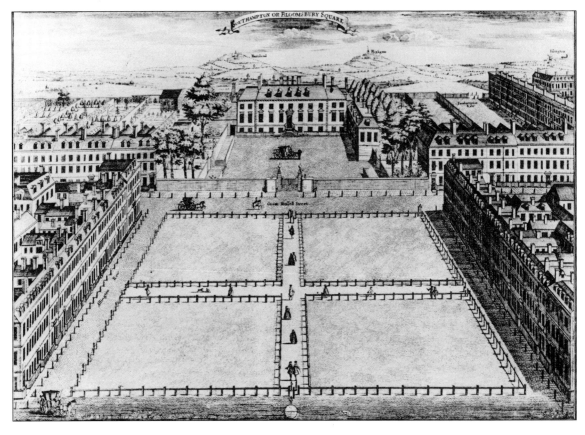

7. *Rachel, Lady Russell. From the painting by Sir Peter Lely at Woburn Abbey*

8. *John, 4th Duke of Bedford, from the painting by Thomas Gainsborough at Woburn Abbey.*

years. In 1683 her husband was implicated in the Rye House Plot against the throne. No traitor but an ardent anti-Catholic, Lord William Russell was executed in Lincoln's Inn Fields, despite his wife's spirited support of his defence when he went on trial for his life.

Bedford House, as it was now called, enjoyed its heyday under John, the business-like and politically active fourth Duke of Bedford (1710-1771). Gouty but good-humoured and a country-lover by temperament, he embellished the garden of Bedford House with groves of limes and acacias, had the gravel walks relaid and installed a greenhouse to grow melons. The house itself was adorned by no less than twenty-four paintings by Canaletto and a further seven by Sir James Thornhill, Hogarth's father-in-law. In 1742 a new line of elmwood pipes was laid across the fields behind the house to bring in its water supply. Baths, both hot and cold, were installed at some date before 1758 and two water closets by 1771. The street in front of the house was repaved but the Duke's official duties and extensive interest in the East India and Greenland trades left him little leisure to undertake further improvements to his London properties. It was left to his widow, the able and assertive Gertrude Leveson Gower, to begin the transformation of the area in the decade after his death.

THE GRANDEES

In 1675 a seven-acre plot of land to the west of Southampton House was granted to Ralph Montagu, who had married Elizabeth, Rachel's younger stepsister. Here, Montagu House was built to the designs of the eminent mathematician, Robert Hooke, and embellished by the hand of the king's own painter, Antonio Verrio. Evelyn thought it 'stately and ample' and most 'nobly furnished' but criticised the garden as 'fine, but too much exposed.' The new house was burnt down in 1686 and although it was rebuilt even more gorgeously to the designs of a French architect, Pierre Puget, it was never regularly used by its owners. In 1739 it was even offered, and seriously considered, as a possible home for the Foundling Hospital before finally becoming the first home of the British Museum.

Around 1680 these two great mansions at the eastern end of Great Russell Street were joined by Thanet House, which still stands, much altered and divided, as Nos. 100, 101 and 102, near the western end. This was occupied by the Earl of Thanet and his son-in-law, the Earl of Leicester, until 1759 and then by the Duke of Bedford's eldest son, the Marquis of Tavistock, until 1785.

To the east of these three virtual palaces was built Powis House, on a site just off where Great Ormond Street joins Queen's Square. Named for its builder, the second Duke of Powis, who was imprisoned in

9. *Montagu House from the north (garden) front. Published by Robert Wilkinson in 1815.*

10. *Powis House, 1714..*

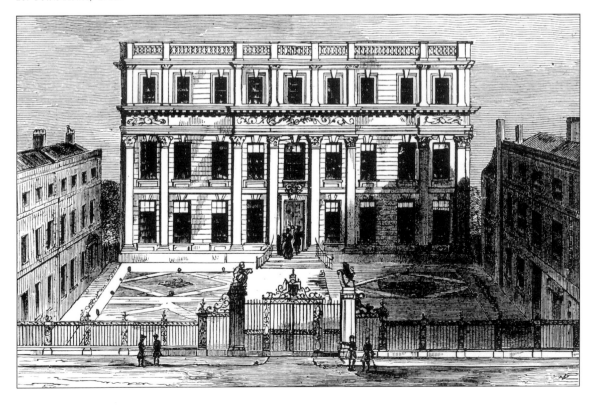

11. Thanet House, drawn by George Scharf.

the Tower for alleged Jacobite sympathies, it was burned down in 1714 (probably an act of arson), when it was occupied by the French Ambassador. Louis XIV paid for a magnificent reconstruction and it subsequently became the residence of the Spanish Ambassador before being demolished in 1777.

In his *Survey of London* (1720) Strype refers to Great Russell Street as:

'inhabited by the Nobility and Gentry, especially the North side, as having Gardens behind the Houses; and the prospect of the pleasant fields up to Hamsted

and Highgate. Insomuch that this Place by Physicians is esteemed the most healthful of any in London.'

The 'pleasant fields' were mostly under the astute management of a dairy-farmer, a Mr Capper, whose passing in 1736 was significant enough to be noted in the *Gentlemen's Magazine*. Mr.Capper's son took holy orders and became a lecturer at the new parish church of St.George's.

In 1756 London's first by-pass, the so-called 'New Road' (now known at this point as the Euston Road), was cut along the northern edge of the Bloomsbury estate. One of its purposes was to enable drovers coming from the west and north-west to herd their cattle and sheep to sale and slaughter at Smithfield without inconveniencing the inhabitants of Oxford Street and Holborn. The Duke of Bedford unsuccessfully raised objections in Parliament on behalf of himself and his tenants, citing dust pollution as an inevitable by-product of the new traffic. Unable to stop the road itself he evidently soon found it so convenient that he upgraded a traditional trackway, running from the back of his house up to the new thoroughfare, into a private road for his own use. (The short Duke's Road, which runs behind St.Pancras New Church, is a remnant of this.)

The existence of this handy route no doubt encouraged the building in 1763 of another substantial

12. 'A Plan of the New Road from Padington to Islington'. It will be seen that the direct route A-D, no doubt preferred, would have run south of the eventual line, cutting a swathe through the northern part of Bloomsbury.

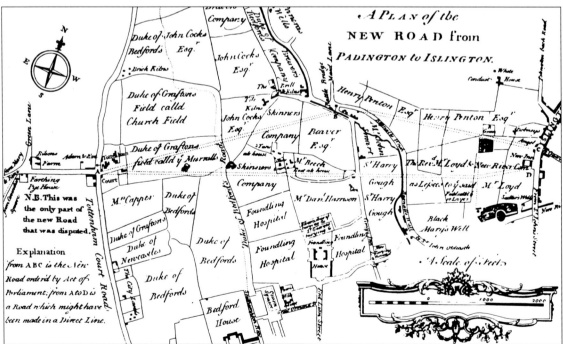

13. *Cartoon by George Cruikshank of St Pancras Fields, for Woodford's* Eccentric Excursions.

mansion which stood on the site of the Hotel Russell. It was originally named for its first occupant, the seventh and last Lord Baltimore, a rake who decamped abroad after being narrowly acquitted of the abduction and rape of a local milliner. Baltimore House then became Bolton House when the Duke of Bolton took up residence. He was succeeded by Lord Loughborough - whose death George III memorialised with the observation "He has not left a greater knave behind him in all my dominions."

THE FIELDS BENEATH

'The town is simply disguised countryside' observes Gillian Tindall in *The Fields Beneath*, her skilful uncovering of the hidden history of Kentish Town. Few urban landscapes could be more urbane than Bloomsbury, with its long, straight streets and neatly planted squares. True and not true, Professor Pevsner notes acidly, for the squares all differ in size and shape 'which is just what distinguishes them from any similar layout that a French architect might have designed.'

14. *Duelling behind Montagu House. An illustration drawn by W.M. Thackeray for his novel* The Virginians.

The site on which Bloomsbury is built consists of a rich loam, under which lay brickearth, then gravel and underneath all, impermeable London clay. This combination held much water and rendered the surface naturally marshy, creating ponds and streams which had to be drained or canalised by ditches. 'Blemund's Dyke', a watercourse probably constructed by the son of the original Blemund, is mentioned in various deeds of the thirteenth century and was still traceable along the southern boundary of Bloomsbury six centuries later, though by then it had become the common sewer. In the thirteenth century also what is now Great Russell Street was referred to as 'the Green Lane'; it then cut through open fields, connecting the original manor house with what is now Tottenham Court Road. Although much of the land to the north of this manor house was pasture and meadow used for grazing, there was also an 'Otefeld' (oat-field) in the Gordon Square area and a 'Vine croft' and large cherry orchard near the house itself. By the sixteenth century there were also specialised gardens for the growing of roses and medicinal herbs and a bowling green for amusement.

A FIELD FOR SPORT

The third chapter of Macaulay's *History of England* includes a description of London in 1685 in which he refers to the fields north of Great Russell Street as 'a vast area renowned... for peaches and snipes.' As his own father's house stood in Great Ormond Street and he knew the area well this apparently idyllic description cannot be dismissed as fanciful. As late as the 1790s peaches, grapes and nectarines were being grown in the back-gardens of houses along Gower Street.

In 1719 the Men of London took on the Men of Kent at cricket in Lamb's Conduit fields, playing for a purse of sixty pounds. More than fifty years after that J.T.Smith, an early employee of the British Museum, and author of a *Book for a Rainy Day* (1845), went on a sketching expedition up to St Pancras Old Church on the north side of the New Road. As he remembered it, the entire way between Great Russell Street and his destination consisted of open fields. This was not quite true. The emptiness was bisected by the elmwood pipeline of the New River Company which brought fresh water to the capital from Hertfordshire. At various points the pipe was raised above the ground on supports and its occasional leakage nourished luxuriant beds of watercress beneath it.

Kite-flying was one of the more innocent pastimes associated with this area but local historian Dobie tut-tutted that:

'In 1800 these fields lay waste and useless .... the resort of depraved wretches, whose amusements consisted chiefly in fighting pitched battles and other disorderly sports, especially on the sabbath day.'

Lord Eldon, the ferocious Lord Chancellor, testified that savage dog-fights were held on a patch of waste-ground just beyond the back-garden of his official residence in Bedford Square.

More decorous leisure was represented by the Toxophilite Society which, in the 1790s, rented the land which now lies between Birkbeck College and the School of Oriental and African Studies and used it for archery practice. They gave up their ground in 1805 as the new Bloomsbury grew up around them.

Around the edges of the fields there were public houses where wayfarers and sportsmen could find refreshment. The present Museum Tavern building in Great Russell Street dates from 1855, but it stands on the site of a hostelry which goes back to 1683, when it was known as the Dog and Duck; given the popularity of the area with wild-fowlers this was an entirely appropriate name. Many more taverns of a low order - The Turk's Head, The Hare and Hounds, The Rat's Castle - were to be found in Dyott Street, which ran at right angles across what is now New Oxford Street. Isolated among the fields towards the northern edge of Bloomsbury, where Cromer Street now runs, was the ramshackle Boot Inn which had a bowling green attached to it and an ice-well. During the Gordon Riots of 1780 it is held to have served as the 'headquarters' of the mob in this locality.

15. *The Boot Inn, Cromer Street.*

A LEGEND AND A LEGACY

In his *Book for a Rainy Day* (1845) J.T. Smith records what was evidently by his day a well-told story about the famed 'Field of Forty Foot Steps' and an incident alleged to have taken place in the reign of Charles II:

'... two brothers were in love with a lady, who would not declare a preference for either, but coolly sat upon a bank to witness the termination of a duel, which proved fatal to both. The bank, it is said, on which she sat, and the footmarks of the brothers, never produced grass again.' Smith explains unromantically 'the fact is these steps were so often trodden that it was impossible for the grass to grow.' The details of the story and the exact location of the site were long a matter of dispute, with the area just north of where the University Senate House now stands being most commonly favoured. Jane Porter in her novel *The Field of the Forty Footsteps* (1828) put the site further to the east, but by the time she was writing the area was already covered by bricks and mortar.

(In 1830 a melodrama of the same title, by Percy Farren, a lesser scion of a distinguished theatrical dynasty, was first performed in a theatre in Tottenham Street, off Tottenham Court Road: see *Illustrations* 16 and 17.)

J.T. Smith's memoir of rural Bloomsbury was paralleled in the 1930s when another local inhabitant, the historian, Eliza Jeffries Davies, painstakingly researched the history of the site over which the University was then rapidly expanding. She, too, emphasised the long continuity with an obscured rural heritage which underlies the scene we see today:

'The admirable plan of Bloomsbury.... subtly interweaving seven garden squares.... is not the creation of one mind or even of one period.... underlying it is a pattern far more ancient. The diversity in the sizes and shapes of the squares is largely due to that of

16. *A theatre bill for Tottenham Street Theatre, January 1830. A member of the cast (playing Peter Pipkin) is the author of the play (see Illustration 17), and Sir Nicholas Vere is played by Mr Gattie (see Illustration 177)*

immemorial fields and closes. The long throughfare near its northeast edge replaced a footpath in that quarter sanctioned in the fourteenth century. And the pleasant orientation follows the lines of one of the oldest thoroughfares in the London area, and of a green lane leading to a medieval manorhouse.'

17. The front cover of The Field of Forty Footsteps *by Percy Farren, c1830.*

Captain Coram's Children

CORAM'S CRUSADE

Cold, clever, calculating Bloomsbury has another side to it - the care and compassion represented by Thomas Coram (1668-1751), shipwright and merchant turned child-care pioneer. Born the son of a ship's captain, Coram spent the years from 1694 to 1704 in Boston and Taunton, Massachusetts, managing shipyards for a consortium of London merchants. Returning to settle in Rotherhithe, he travelled daily to work in the City and was constantly distressed by the sight of abandoned infants, left dead or dying in the streets. In 1722 he mooted the idea of forming a non-profit joint-stock company to run a hostel for such children, but coming in the aftermath of the collapse of the speculation of the South Sea Bubble it was an untimely notion and

nothing came of it. Undeterred, Coram changed tack and began to canvass among the aristocracy for signatures to petition the king for a Royal Charter to establish such a home. At first he met such stony indifference that he felt he could no more persuade the great and the good to take up his cause than 'to putt downe their Breeches and present their Backsides to the King and Queen'. Perhaps they were dissuaded by the argument put about by opponents of his project, that it would only serve as a positive encouragement to immorality, acting

> '*To encourage the progress of vulgar Amours,*
> *The breeding of rogues and th'encreasing of Whores.*'

A decisive step forward came in 1729 thanks to the sympathy of a group of ladies 'of Quality and Distinction', many of whom were young enough to understand the plight of unmarried mothers less fortunately placed than themselves. The petition they agreed to support did not mince words but condemned in outrage the 'frequent Murders upon poor Miserable Infant Children at their Birth' and the 'Inhumane Custom of exposing New-born children to Perish in the streets or the putting out of such

18. *'An exact Representation of the Form and Manner in which EXPOSED and DESERTED Young children are Admitted into the FOUNDLING HOSPITAL'. This scene, depicted in 1749, shows a lady on the right holding a white ball, by which her child is admitted. The woman second from the left has a black ball and is rejected, and a third is drawing from the bag.*

19. *Captain Thomas Coram, by B. Nebot.*

20. *View of the Hospital and its grounds, 1751.*

unhappy Foundlings to wicked and barbarous Nurses.' As a remedy the petition proposed 'an Hospital after the example of France, Holland and other Christian Countrys.... for the Reception, Maintenance and proper Education of such abandoned helpless infants.' In 1737 George II finally accepted Coram's petition and called for a provisional list of governors to oversee the new home. These were to include the popular painter, William Hogarth, and the fashionable sculptor, Michael Rysbrack. In 1739 a Royal Charter was finally granted to a 'Hospital for the Maintenance and Education of Exposed and Deserted Young Children'.

It took a further two years to draw up a plan of administration, appoint staff and find suitable ac-commodation and it was not until 1741 that the Foundling Hospital finally opened its doors in Hatton Garden.

In that very year Coram's wife died and the child-less old man, now in his seventies, went quickly to pieces. When he dared to criticise two of the governors and the hospital's head nurse he was himself ousted from his official position and reduced to haunting the institution he had so long campaigned for with pockets full of ginger-bread to give to the children. So low did his condition fall that in 1749 the Prince of Wales and a group of City merchants clubbed together to give him a decent annual allowance. He died two years later, having failed to establish a second Foundling Hospital in Westminster.

A HOME FOR THE HOSPITAL

At the outset it was the set policy to ask no questions regarding the background of any child presented. The attempt to operate on a 'first come, first served' basis quickly broke down as a result of disorderly scenes among disappointed applicants. In 1742 a balloting system was introduced. Each applicant drew a ball from a leather bag: white secured admission, black rejection and red a 'standby' place in case an admitted child should prove to have an infectious illness. Although diseased infants were resolutely turned away, a third of those admitted in the first year died anyway. Nevertheless the number of applicants soon far outran the number of places and more restrictive conditions were imposed. A child had to be under twelve months old and the first born to an unmarried mother of previously good reputation, deserted by the father. To shield infants from the danger of infection inherent in city life they were sent to foster-parents in the country for their first four or five years, then brought back to London to be educated. Even so the need for larger and more appropriate accommodation soon became very evident.

In 1745 the Governors bought 55 acres of ground in Lamb's Conduit Fields. Here they erected, to the designs of Theodore Jacobsen, a home, complete with a chapel, where Coram himself was buried. The inscription on his tomb proclaimed him to be 'a man eminent in the most eminent virtue, the love of mankind' and promised that 'his name will never want a monument as long as this Hospital shall subsist.' (He now lies buried in St. Andrew's, Holborn.)

By 1756 1,384 children had been admitted and in the same year a Parliamentary grant enabled the Hospital to extend its catchment area far beyond the capital. This 'general reception' policy attracted 425 children in the first month alone. Many recruits were dead on arrival and so, to avoid providing an easy mode of disposing of murdered infants, a token of their mother's identity was required to accompany all newcomers. Over the years the Hospital built up a collection of miscellaneous trinkets, including cards, lockets, book-marks and even lottery tickets, which were used to identify the foundlings.

By 1760 another 15,000 children had been accepted - of these less than a third lived long enough to proceed to apprenticeship or placement in domestic service. Government support was withdrawn in that same year. The Governors thereupon decided to accept any waif accompanied by a bank-note for £100, a policy that lasted until 1801. By then the development of the open land around the Hospital had secured it a new source of income.

The policy of the Hospital was to maintain a strict segregation between boys and girls. Only on Christmas Day were they allowed to mix and even in death they were divided, buried in separate cemeteries.

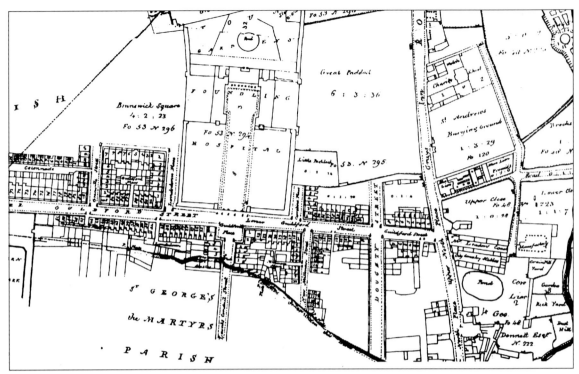

21. *Part of the parish map of St Pancras, by J. Thompson, c1800. The Foundling Hospital and its grounds are in the centre; the estate stretches from the St George burial grounds to the north, to Guilford Street in the south, and to the Grays Inn Road on the east.*

22. William Hogarth.

23. *George Frederick Handel, who conducted numerous performances of* **The Messiah** *in aid of the Foundling Hospital.*

24. *The eastern colonnade of the Hospital.*

25. *The courtyard of the Hospital, c1920.*

26. *The eastern colonnade of the Hospital.*

27. *A Foundling girl, by Harold Copping.*

28. *A Foundling boy, by Harold Copping.*

29. *Children in the Coram's Fields playground, 1930s*

ALL FOR CHARITY

Coram's Hospital became London's most fashionable cause. Its supporters included Hogarth, who painted a masterly portrait of the founder; Handel, who presented an organ to the chapel and presided at benefit performances of *Messiah* which raised over £7,000; and Sir Joshua Reynolds, who arranged private views of new paintings, which eventually became the Royal Academy's annual exhibitions. Charity breakfasts were organised and patronised by ladies of 'quality'. The chapel became a smart place to attend a Sunday service, attracting brilliant preachers, like the witty Sidney Smith and influential worshippers, like Charles Dickens.

Throughout the nineteenth century male 'graduates' of the Hospital were enlisted in the services, placed as clerks or craftsmen or despatched to the colonies; females mostly went into domestic service. Adoption by strangers was not permitted, so that children could be returned to their mothers if they proved able to support them.

The Foundling Hospital gave children not only a home, sustenance and an education but a name as well. Many entrants were named for governors of the Hospital, others for great figures from history (Milton, Cromwell, Chaucer etc.) and others still for famous fictional characters (Tom Jones, Clarissa Harlowe etc.). The last child to be received under the system of parliamentary grants was ironically dubbed 'Kitty Finis'.

The Foundling Hospital finally left Bloomsbury in 1926 and settled in new quarters at Berkhamsted in 1935. A handsome neo-Georgian building at 40 Brunswick Square now houses the offices of the Thomas Coram Foundation for Children. It contains a Court Room which is an exact reproduction of the original and many of the paintings and treasures donated by supporters over the centuries are still on display there.

Thanks to the exertions of local inhabitants and a timely grant from Lord Rothermere the land where the Hospital once stood was preserved as a much-valued open space - Coram's Fields - where adults may enter only if accompanied by a child.

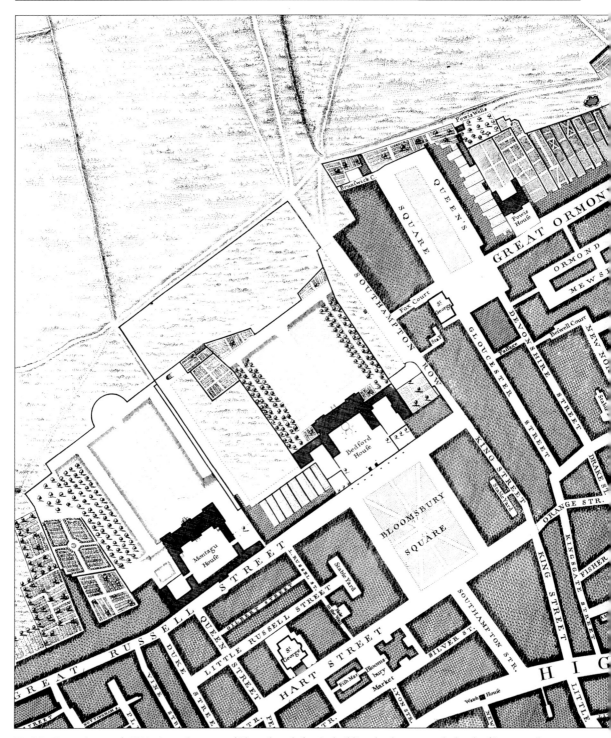

30. *John Rocque's map of c1746 shows the extent of Bloomsbury before its building development at the hands of Leverton, Burton and Cubitt. Montagu and Bedford Houses still look out across fields to Hampstead, and Queen Square, with only one side developed, is the northern outpost.*

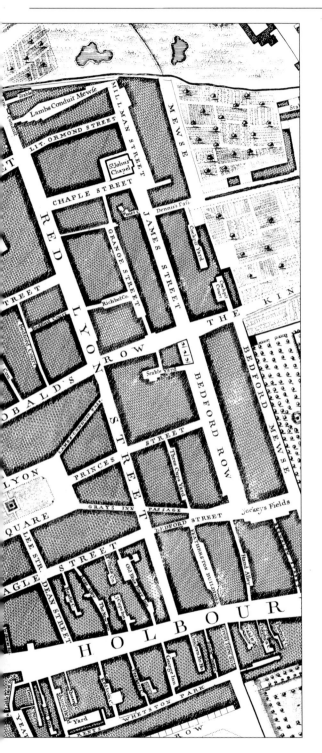

The Building of Bloomsbury

THE REGULATION OF SPECULATION

The area now thought of as Bloomsbury, and in particular the area north of Great Russell Street and Theobald's Road, was essentially built up during the last quarter of the eighteenth century and the first half of the next.

This meant that the building conventions and constructional standards were governed, at least in theory and to a very large extent in practice, by the provisions of the Building Act of 1774, drafted by sculptor and City Sheriff, Sir Robert Taylor and City Surveyor, George Dance the Younger. This act aimed to ensure that even ordinary houses would be as sound and fireproof as possible. House-types were categorised into four bands or 'rates', depending on their value and floor area (excluding out-buildings). A 'First Rate' house would be worth more than £850 and occupy more than nine 'squares of building' (i.e. 900 sq.ft.); a 'Fourth Rate' would be valued at under £150 and occupy less than 350 sq.ft. For each rate detailed specifications for foundations, party walls, external walls etc. were laid down. The result was minimum standards for urban housing, though with a real risk that uniformity meant monotony. Dance himself was to have his last home in Gower Street but the 1849 *Handbook of London* was still to dismiss the entire thoroughfare as 'a dull, heavy street of third-rate houses.'

BEGINNING IN BEDFORD SQUARE

The Act of 1774 coincided with a surge of building in the West End, which included the construction of Portman and Manchester Squares and Portland Place and, in Bloomsbury, Bedford Square. Back in 1766 the fourth Duke of Bedford, a great admirer of the King's Circus in Bath, had announced his intention to create a Bedford Circus on his London estate, but nothing had come of it by his death in 1771 and it was left to his formidable widow, Lady Gertrude Leveson-Gower and his estate agent, Robert Palmer, to push the scheme forward. Building agreements were signed with William Scott and Robert Crews in 1776, despite the outbreak of war in the American colonies and a consequent rise in building costs.

Bedford Square is one of modern London's greatest architectural treasures, because it survives closer to its original condition than any creation of Inigo Jones or Robert Adam. If it did have what one might call an overall designer it was Thomas Leverton (who lived at No.13 from 1795 to 1824), but the acute eye of Sir John Soane accurately detected that it was

31. *A last look at Bedford House on the northern side of Bloomsbury Square - it was pulled down c1800. Drawing by Edward Dayes, 1787.*

32. *Queen Square, also in 1787, looking towards the open aspect to the north.*

33 & 34. *Two views of the east side of Bedford Square in 1851, by T.H. Shepherd. The top looks north, the bottom looks south.*

35. *Bedford Square; postcard c1905*

36. *Thomas Leverton*

essentially a product of the 'spirit of speculation'. Nevertheless it incorporated such distinctive stylistic features as bold door-surrounds made from artificial Coade stone and ceilings decorated by the noted Swiss artist, Angelica Kauffmann.

Gower Street came next, from about 1790 onwards. Pevsner praises its 'almost wholly unadorned brick terraces, even, soothing, dignified, and with a sense of overall planning', though even he does concede that it is 'certainly without much imagination'.

THE FOUNDLING ESTATE

The development of the Bedford estate began to falter around 1790 and the initiative passed to the governors of the Foundling Hospital, which still stood amid some fifty acres of open land. Their decision to exploit this space was a controversial one and so far divided them that a faction even went to court to try to prevent the whole enterprise. Some opposed the destruction of a pleasant amenity, while others feared the creation of a shoddy slum that would endanger the children's health. Supporters of the scheme, however, were lured on by the prospect of a healthy rental income which would at last set the institution's finances on a solid basis.

In the event a development plan was drawn up by Samuel Pepys Cockerell. He suggested laying out on either side of the existing Hospital building the spaces now known as Brunswick Square and Mecklenburgh

Square. These would not only preserve the institution's open aspect but also supply the sort of architectural ambience which would raise rather than depress 'the character of this Hospital itself as an Object of National Munificence.' If a large-scale development was to be completed without throwing undue strain on the resources of the Hospital itself Cockerell foresaw the need to offer scope for the participation of small-scale speculative builders and therefore proposed that the houses should be of all classes, ranging from the First to the Fourth Rate. He also saw the need to proceed by self-financing stages.

The 1790s proved to be a difficult time for any development, no matter how cautiously envisaged, for Britain was once more plunged into war, this time with revolutionary France; it was to last a quarter of a century.

Against a background of rising prices Cockerell had considerable problems in enforcing standards on the sub-contractors who had been assigned building leases. In the end he was sacked - then indirectly reinstated as a consultant to oversee the work of his star pupil, Joseph Kay. It was Kay who was to design the handsome east terrace of Mecklenburgh Square.

It was the original intention of the Foundling Hospital governors to spread the work (and therefore the risks of failure) among a large number of developers, but one soon rose to dominate the entire enterprise: by 1802 James Burton had built almost 600 houses on the estate and was looking for wider fields to conquer - or build over.

BURTON'S BLOOMSBURY

In 1800 the Duke of Bedford employed Burton to pull down Bedford House and cover its site with the houses that now form the north side of Bloomsbury Square, the south side of Russell Square and the street joining them, Bedford Place. The lay-out of Russell Square's gardens was entrusted to Humphry Repton (1752-1818), England's foremost landscape architect. Burton, meanwhile, went ahead with building the western side of the Square and the eastern side of Tavistock Square. As Sir John Summerson has stressed, most of the joinery and iron-work for these terraces was mass-produced, so 'an individual Bloomsbury house would be a matter of assembly rather than design.'

Whatever their aesthetic shortcomings Burton's buildings were more than welcomed as they went up. Antiquary and local resident, J.P. Malcolm, devoted ten pages of his *Londinium Redivivium* (1803) to the 'Increase of London', singling out Burton for special commendation:

'The present war has been a great check to the enterprising spirit of builders; consequently the improvements have been nearly confined to the North-

37. *Brunswick Square, developed by the Foundling Hospital. Photograph in the 1920s.*

38. *James Burton, from a mezzotint.*

39. Russell Square with the statue of the Duke of Bedford. The main attraction, however, is a Punch and Judy show. From a watercolour by T.H. Shepherd.

ern side of the metropolis, and have chiefly been in the hands of one eminent builder, Mr. Burton. The grounds are those belonging to the Foundling Hospital and the Duke of Bedford... Perhaps, in these times of difficulty and distress, no plan has a more beneficial effect than thus employing so many hands, which would otherwise have been idle. When the excessive price of every article is considered, what heart is there but must rejoice at the busy scene this neighbourhood presents and bless the proprietors.'

Burton's energy was by no means confined to Bloomsbury (he was Nash's main collaborator in developing Regent Street) nor even to building. In 1804, when Britain lay under threat of invasion, 'Colonel Burton' raised a thousand-strong regiment of 'Loyal British Artificers', officered by architects and foremen, who drilled along the unbuilt edges of the new town they were creating. In 1807 he leased from the Skinners' Company a patch of land which lay north-east of the Foundling estate and built Burton Street and Burton (now Cartwright) Crescent and a villa for himself where the BMA headquarters now stands. Burton's interest in Bloomsbury ended in 1817. Having made a fortune there he lost it in trying to develop St. Leonards-on-Sea, where he died in 1837.

CUBITT'S BLOOMSBURY

Burton's successor as the presiding daemon of Bloomsbury's development was Thomas Cubitt (1788-1855), an organiser of genius, who, by the age of thirty, had done what no other master-builder had ever done before - created a business with its own permanent paid labour-force of craftsmen and its own permanent workshops and materials yards (in both Gray's Inn Road and Pimlico). Having begun by building barracks and port facilities on government contract during the Napoleonic wars, Cubitt had gone on to master the more difficult art of arranging his own contracts, juggling the necessary components of a successful speculation - land, labour, capital, materials and designs - to keep his men in continuous employment by building large chunks of Highbury, Stoke Newington, Barnsbury, Belgravia and Pimlico.

Cubitt turned his attention to Bloomsbury in the 1820s, completing Tavistock Square and going on to build Woburn Place, part of Gordon Square, the streets that lead off them and the charming shopping parade now known as Woburn Walk. Being able to offer craftsmen permanent employment, he could pick the best; buying materials on a huge scale he could set similarly high standards. Cubitt's houses therefore represented a level of style and quality unprecedented among speculative builders. He was still building in Bloomsbury at the time of his death, Taviton Street and Gordon Square being completed by his executors. One of these was his younger brother, Lewis, who designed King's Cross station and who, from 1849 to 1867, lived at 53 Bedford Square.

40. *Thomas Cubitt.*

41. *Houses in Frederick Street, just around the corner from Cubitt's yard, and built by him.*

42. *The extent of Bloomsbury as shown on Richard Horwood's map at the beginning of the 19th century.*

Worship and Belief

TWO ST GEORGE'S

Bloomsbury's religious history begins with the establishment of the church of St.George the Martyr in Queen Square as a chapel-of-ease to St Andrew's, Holborn in 1706; in 1723 it was promoted to the status of a parish church as a result of the development of the Bloomsbury area. The rector from 1747 to 1765 was the antiquarian, William Stukeley, who was chiefly responsible for the erroneous beliefs that Stonehenge was a Druidic temple and that a large Roman settlement had once existed near the old church of St. Pancras. The church was drastically altered by S.S. Teulon in 1868.

In 1713 two parallel plots were purchased to serve as burial grounds for St. George the Martyr and St. George's, Hart Street (now Bloomsbury Way) which was then under construction. Robert Nelson, religious pamphleteer and a leading member of the Society for the Promotion of Christian Knowledge, was the first person to be interred here, in 1715. The historian Timbs, noting the reluctance of locals to use the facility before Nelson's interment, whimsically interpreted this as a crucial turning-point in its acceptability - 'people like to be buried in company, and in good company.' Nelson was later joined by a number of Jacobites, executed after the abortive rising of 1745 to put Bonnie Prince Charlie on the throne and, less picturesquely, by Nancy Dawson 'the celebrated horn-pipe dancer of Covent Garden'. Timbs does not note the impact of these more colourful newcomers. The burial ground was closed in 1855 and in 1884 the portion assigned to St George's, Bloomsbury was opened as a public garden; the other half was added to it in 1889.

The church of St George, Hart Street, was built from the funds provided by the Fifty New Churches Act of 1711; but it was not completed until 1731 - at more than three times the estimated cost. The architect was Wren's great protege, Nicholas Hawksmoor. Pevsner praises it as having 'perhaps the most grandiose of London's eighteenth century church fronts, with all Hawksmoor's vigour but without his oddities.' Alastair Service notes the sophisticated internal plan which enables the altar to be placed in its traditional eastern position, although the site itself runs north-south.

Contemporaries, however, were far more interested in the church's unique steeple, a stepped pyramid, allegedly based on Pliny's fanciful description of the Mausoleum of Halicarnassus (remnants of which may be seen in the British Museum) and topped by a statue of George I in a Roman toga, the gift of Mr.William Huck, a loyal and royal brewer.

43. St George the Martyr church, Queen Square. From Chamberlain's History of London (1770)

44. William Stukeley

The connoisseur, Horace Walpole, sneered at this exuberance as 'a masterpiece of absurdity'. A much-quoted squib summarised popular amusement:

'When Henry VIII left the Pope in the lurch,
The Protestants made him head of the church,
But George's good subjects, the Bloomsbury people,
Instead of the Church, made him head of the steeple.'

45. *St George's, Bloomsbury; by Thomas Malton, 1799.*

G.E. Street restored the church sympathetically in 1870 but a London guide book of 1876 still dismissed it as 'the most pretentious and ugliest edifice in the metropolis.'

There were other, smaller, institutions to serve local worshippers in the area - Baptist chapels in Eagle Street, Keppel Street and John Street; the Episcopal Chapel of St. John near Great James Street; and the Bedford Chapel in Bloomsbury Street, whose lease expressly forbade its use for marriages, christenings, the churching of women or prayer for the sick.

PRIESTS, PROPHETS AND FRAUDS

If Bloomsbury has, on the whole been more productive of sceptics than of saints, it has still been the home of a number of significant religious figures, invariably outside the mainstream of conventional Anglicanism.

The controversial, charismatic Richard Baxter (1615-91) lived briefly in Bloomsbury Square in 1681. Cursed by ill-health throughout his life he yet proved himself a brilliant preacher, a dedicated pastor and a prolific pamphleteer, publishing some two hundred works.

Bishop Richard Challoner (1691-1781) Vicar Apostolic to London's beleaguered Catholic community during the difficult years when 'anti-Papist' bigotry was at its height, lived in Lamb's Conduit Street and died in Old Gloucester Street. His main scholarly achievement was the 'Douai Bible' used by English-speaking Catholics.

In 1814 the crazed, illiterate prophetess, Joanna Southcott, announced to her followers that, although she was in her sixties she was about to give birth to the Saviour. She swelled visibly, took to her bed and died of dropsy.

The irreverent Reverend Sydney Smith (1771-1845) lived at 14 (then No.8) Doughty Street and 77 Guilford Street while serving as preacher at the Foundling Hospital. A man who defined his idea of heaven as 'eating *pate de foie gras* to the sound of trumpets' might be expected to be more popular among wits than with his ecclesiastical superiors and so it proved. Admitting ruefully that 'the whole of my life has passed like a razor - in hot water or a scrape', he

47. Rev. Sydney Smith

46. Joanna Southcott

48. Cardinal Newman.

In the present century Bloomsbury has provided a home for some characters of decidedly more marginal spiritual quality. Torrington Square served as a base for Ignatius Trebich-Lincoln whose colourful career took him from rabbi to Buddhist priest via Anglican clergyman and Liberal MP. At 99 Gower Street, which is now part of the Catholic Chaplaincy, a 'Temple of the Occult' provided a cover for the troilist philanderings of its proprietorial spirit, who was eventually brought down by his penchant for stealing from his victims. 28 Bernard Street provided a metropolitan bolt-hole where the Rector of Stiffkey, Norfolk, could pass his weekdays and nights conspicuously failing to save fallen women. After a sensational defrocking trial and a period exhibiting himself in a barrel at Blackpool, he was to be eaten alive by a lion in the course of another stunt.

MORE CHURCHES

The rapid development of the Bloomsbury area in the first quarter of the nineteenth century prompted another burst of church-building.

St Pancras New Church, designed by Henry and William Inwood, was the first to be built in the newly-fashionable Greek Revival style. Modelled on Henry Inwood's sketches of the Erectheum on Ath-

observed to his conventional and successful brother 'You and I are exceptions to the laws of nature; you have risen by your gravity and I have sunk by my levity.'

Controversialist John Henry Newman (1801-90), whose defection from the reformist Oxford Movement led him eventually to Catholicism and a Cardinal's cap, passed his childhood years at 17 Southampton Place. The author of the hymn *Lead Kindly Light* , he also wrote a classic defence of his religious beliefs - *Apologia pro Vita Sua* - as well as *The Dream of Gerontius* (which Elgar set to music), and *The Idea of a University*. Cardinal Manning summarised him as 'a great hater' and Lytton Strachey gave him a good pummelling in *Eminent Victorians*.

Ram Mohun Roy (1772-1833) Hindu scholar, educationalist and journalist, lived in Bedford Square while visiting England to plead for improvements in British rule in India. A vigorous campaigner against suttee (widow-burning) and founder of the reformist movement Brahmo Samaj (Society of the Supreme Being), he was deeply influenced by Christianity and especially by Unitarianism. Welcomed by William IV and feted by Unitarians, he was taken fatally ill visiting Unitarian friends in Bristol, where he is buried. The first great moderniser of the Indian intellectual heritage, he is ranked beside Gandhi as a father of his nation.

49. Invitation to the consecration of St Pancras church in 1822

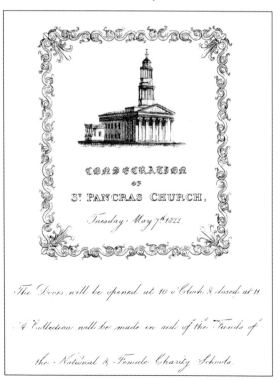

50. *St Pancras church, 1822; by Thomas Kearnan.*

51. *Catholic Apostolic church, Gordon Square.*

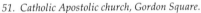

ens' Acropolis, and complete with caryatids, it was the most expensive church-building project of its time. The Inwoods followed this effort almost immediately with another Greek creation, St Peter, Regent Square, built between 1824 and 1826. The Scottish Presbyterian Church, built over the same period and in the same square, was designed by William Tite, future architect of the Royal Exchange; in complete contrast it was modelled on York Minster.

Christ Church, Woburn Square, built between 1831 and 1833 and designed by Vulliamy, followed Wren's favourite interior layout of a Greek cross, but was Gothic in external decoration. The New Jerusalem Church was built in Argyle Square in an Anglo-Norman style in 1844 for the use of the Swedenborgians.

All these buildings were literally overshadowed in 1853 by the construction of the Catholic & Apostolic Church in Gordon Square to accommodate the Irvingites, a sect founded by the charismatic Edward Irving after his expulsion from the Presbyterian church in Regent Square for encouraging his followers to 'speak in tongues' - i.e. babble spontaneously,

52. *St Peter's, Regent Square; by Thomas H. Shepherd, 1826.*

53. The National Scotch Church, Regent Square; by Thomas H. Shepherd, 1829.

supposedly in ancient Biblical languages, in a state alleged to be one of divine possession. Charlotte Eliot was one member of his congregation thus gifted, or afflicted; she composed over a hundred hymns before being received into the Roman church.

Conceived on a cathedral scale by Raphael Brandon, the 'Irvingite' church was originally intended to have a tower and spire 300 foot high - which would have been easily the tallest in London - had it been built. It is now the University Church of Christ the King.

Irving's wayward example was followed by Noel, the minister of the Episcopal Chapel of St John, who could attract congregations big enough to jam the street outside with their carriages. In 1848 he seceded from the established church and transferred his mission to the Baptist chapel in John Street, leaving the scene of his former glories to the demolition men.

Holy Cross Roman Catholic Church in Cromer Street was built in 1867 and has no tower at all.

54. *Tavistock Chapel, Tavistock Place.*

55. *Christ Church, Woburn Square.*

A RAINBOW OF FAITHS

Despite the agnostic atmosphere represented by such Bloomsbury spirits as Jeremy Bentham and Herbert Spencer, the area has long housed the headquarters of religious organisations representing a truly ecumenical spectrum of beliefs. John Street alone in the mid-nineteenth century was home to the offices of the South American Missionary Society, the 'Open Air Mission' and the Africa Inland Mission. The Swedenborg Society, established in 1805 to propagate the views of the Swedish mystic, Count Swedenborg, initially settled at 36 Bloomsbury Street before moving to Bloomsbury Way. The present century has seen the addition of Salvation Army premises in Judd Street; Friends' House (1925-7), the Quaker headquarters on the Euston Road; and the Jewish Museum and court of the Chief Rabbi in Tavistock Square (1932). And what is now the British Medical Association headquarters on the eastern side of Tavistock Square was originally built for the Theosophical Society. Great Russell Street is home to the headquarters of the Buddhist Society, Great James Street houses the offices of the Ismaili Institute and St Mary's German Lutheran church is to be found in Sandwich Street.

Entrance of the British Museum, from

56. *Views of the south and north fronts of Montagu House when first used by the British Museum.*

The British Museum

A BARGAIN BEQUEST

The British Museum originated in the offer of a Bloomsbury resident, royal physician and President of the Royal Society, Sir Hans Sloane (1660-1753), of his huge collection of antiquities and natural curiosities in exchange for an endowment by Parliament of £20,000 to provide incomes for his daughters after his death. It was a most generous offer, considering that

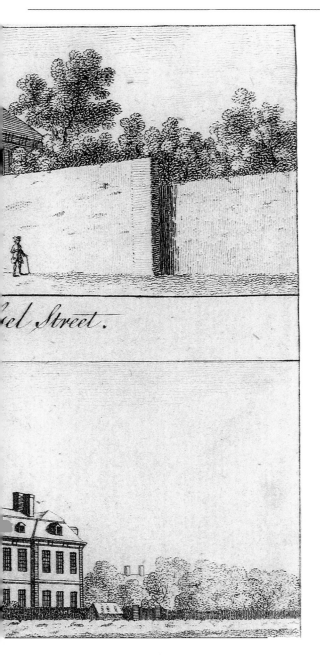

el Street.

57. *Sir Hans Sloane*

the items involved cost Sloane three or four times that sum. An Act passed in the year of Sloane's death duly authorised the purchase of both his collection and an archive of manuscripts accumulated by politician Robert Harley, 1st Earl of Oxford. The Act also provided for the establishment of 'one general repository for the better reception of the said collec-

tions' and for the manuscript collection of the Cotton family, which had been presented to the nation half a century before. A public lottery raised £300,000 to fund the project and in 1755 £10,250 of that sum was paid for the purchase of Montagu House and a further £12,873 spent on its repair.

The museum opened its doors in 1759 - but not very wide. Admission was for three hours a day and only to visitors who had made a written application for an appointment; these were admitted at a rate of no more than ten per hour and were accompanied round in groups of no more than five. Unrestricted access to the galleries was not permitted until 1879.

EXPANDING AND REBUILDING

The core collection grew rapidly through both purchase and gift. In 1757 George II presented the royal library of 10,500 volumes, collected by British monarchs since the reign of Henry VIII. This handsome gesture brought with it the additional right to receive a copy of every new book registered at Stationers' Hall. The defeat of Napoleon's expeditionary force in Egypt in 1801 brought much of his plunder, including the precious Rosetta stone; it took an international effort stretching over a quarter of a century to unlock the secret of its hieroglyphic inscription but eventual success created the new discipline of Egyp

58. *The Hall and Staircase of the British Museum in the old Montagu House. By Pugin and Rowlandson, 1808.*

59. The courtyard of the British Museum after rebuilding.

tology. In 1816 Lord Elgin presented the celebrated marbles which he had brought back from the Parthenon and Erectheum in Athens. (It was the sight of these which inspired Keats' famous *Ode on a Grecian Urn*) Bequests brought the original Mss of the plays of David Garrick, as well as specimens gathered in the South Seas by Captain Cook and Sir Joseph Banks and in Java by Sir Stamford Raffles. Apart from aristocratic and scholarly collectors, corporations like the Bank of England and East India Company also proved to be generous donors.

As the collection continued its relentless expansion temporary structures were erected around Montagu House but by the 1820s it was evident that a major rebuilding programme would be required to store and display it adequately.

Architect Robert Smirke (1781-1867) planned to build on the open ground behind Montagu House, using the house as the south side of a quadrangle with an open courtyard in the middle. An east wing was built between 1823 and 1826 (on the site of the former home of the tragedian Kemble) to take the King's Library; a west wing followed in 1831-4 and a north in 1833-8. Work began on an entirely new front in 1842 and this necessitated the demolition of Montagu House itself. The new Central Hall was opened in 1847.

60. Sir Robert Smirke

THE READING ROOM

By 1850 the library collections were being consulted by 70,000 visitors a year. Between 1852 and 1857, therefore, the central courtyard was converted (by Sydney Smirke, brother of the architect) into a vast domed Reading Room at the suggestion of the Principal Librarian, Sir Anthony Panizzi. At the time of its completion it was the second largest dome in the world, being surpassed only by the Pantheon in Rome. The Reading Room has been used by Dickens, Carlyle, Ruskin, Marx, Hardy, Shaw and Lenin and immortalised in Virginia Woolf's celebrated essay on women writers *A Room of One's Own* - 'one stood under the vast dome, as if one were a thought in the huge bald forehead which is so splendidly encircled by a band of famous names.' Marie Stopes (1880-1958) set herself what one might call a course of purposive reading. Still a virgin after five years of marriage, she aimed to read every single book in the collection relating to sex. In 1918 she published her pioneering sex manual *Married Love* - and married a second husband.

In 1881 the natural history collections were removed to South Kensington and in 1905 the newspaper archive relocated at Colindale. Twentieth-century extensions include the Edward VII galleries at the rear, designed by Sir John Burnet and opened in 1914 and the West Gallery, completed in 1938, to house the Parthenon sculptures.

EXHIBITS AND EMPLOYEES

The Museum's most famous exhibits include the Portland Vase, the Lindisfarne Gospels, the original manuscript of Handel's *Messiah* and two copies of Magna Carta. Twentieth-century acquisitions have included the Saxon treasure-hoard known as the Sutton Hoo ship-burial; the Mildenhall hoard of Roman silverware; an entire mosaic pavement excavated from the ruins of a Roman villa in Devon; the world's oldest printed document, the Diamond Sutra of 868; the log book of Nelson's *Victory*; Scott of the Antarctic's last diary - and original manuscripts of the Beatles' lyrics. The displays also include manuscripts, books and letters by numerous Bloomsbury authors, including Bacon, Cowper, Shelley, Swinburne, Darwin, Christina Rossetti, Thackeray and Conrad.

A number of the employees of the British Museum have won fame in their own right. Inscribed next to the Museum's main entrance is the moving and much-copied epitaph 'For the Fallen' composed by

61. The old Museum Reading Room

62. *Sir Anthony Panizzi, by 'Ape' published in* Vanity Fair, *1874*

63. *Sunlight in the Mausoleum Room. An undated postcard.*

poet Laurence Binyon (1869-1943) who worked in the Department of Prints and Drawings:-

'They shall not grow old,
    as we that are left grow old.
Age shall not weary them,
    nor the years condemn.
At the going down of the sun,
    and in the morning
We shall remember them.'

Arthur Waley (1889-1966), a colleague in the Prints Department, established a unique literary reputation through his elegant translations of Chinese and Japanese classics. Born into a wealthy German-Jewish family named Schloss, he grew up an expert skier and skater but partial blindness rendered him unfit for military service in 1914, the year in which he adopted his mother's maiden name. His anthology

of *A Hundred and Seventy Chinese Poems* fulfilled his hope of appealing 'to people who do not ordinarily read poetry' and went through several editions. His translation of the medieval Japanese *Tale of Genji* won acclaim in Japan itself as a masterpiece. Waley lived quietly in Bloomsbury (36 Endsleigh Street and then 50 Gordon Square) for most of his life, eventually lecturing at the University's School of Oriental Studies and refusing every invitation to visit either of the two countries on whose culture he was an acknowledged world expert. The 'Bloomsbury Group' thought him rather a bore.

Sir Angus Wilson retired from the BM Library in 1955, just before publication of his best-seller *Anglo-Saxon Attitudes*; a satirical novelist, he also wrote studies of Zola, Dickens and Kipling.

Now covering over thirteen acres and employing 1,200 staff, the British Museum receives over four million visitors a year, making it Britain's greatest indoor, non-commercial attraction. Excluding prints

64. The interior of the present Reading Room, as depicted in Edward Walford's Old and New London.

and drawings, its collections include some four million objects. Space therefore remains the problem it has always been. The natural history collections were removed to the new purpose-built Natural History Museum in South Kensington in the 1880s. In 1970 the ethnographic collection moved to the Museum of Mankind in Burlington Gardens. In 1973 the book and manuscript departments were split off to form the British Library and the intention is that this should be removed altogether to a new home by St Pancras station by the end of the present decade.

65. A cartoon depicting the proposed removal of the natural history section of the Museum to Brompton.

71. *The new building of the College of Preceptors in Bloomsbury Square, as depicted in* The Graphic, *2 April, 1887.*

In 1854 a Working Men's College, the brainchild of F.D. Maurice, opened its doors at 31 Red Lion Square for the purpose of providing the humbler classes with an education which would be 'regular and organic, not taking the form of mere miscellaneous lectures.' In 1857 the College moved into 45 Great Ormond Street and eventually took over No.44 as well. In 1864 a Working Women's College opened at 29 Queen Square; one of its co-founders was Barbara Bodichon (1827-91), founder of Britain's first feminist journal, the *English Woman's Journal*. After his death Maurice was succeeded as Principal of the Working Men's College by his disciple, Thomas Hughes, the author of *Tom Brown's Schooldays*.

72. *Frederick Denison Maurice*

73. The Russell Institution in Coram Street; by Thomas H. Shepherd, 1828.

LEARNED SOCIETIES

What became known as the Russell Institution in Coram Street was built by James Burton in 1802, burned down in 1803 and, when rebuilt, established as a literary and scientific club. Its members came to include Thackeray, Dickens and John Leech and it accumulated a library of 16,000 volumes.

The Entomological Society was established at 12 Bedford Row in 1833 and in 1841 the newly-founded Pharmaceutical Society moved into a fine Nash building at 17 Bloomsbury Square. For some years the Society of Biblical Archaeology maintained its offices just round the corner at 11 Hart Street (now Bloomsbury Way). In 1915 the Royal Institute of Chemistry moved into new premises at 30 Russell Square, designed by Sir John Burnet (and commended by Pevsner as 'dignified').

The fine Courtauld collection of Old Master and Impressionist paintings was housed in galleries above the Warburg Institute from the 1950s until the 1990s, when it moved to Somerset House. But the Percival David Foundation of Chinese Art is still housed at 53 Gordon Square; its collection of ceramics is reckoned to be one of the very finest outside China itself. And at 20 Bloomsbury Square there is the Paul Mellon Centre for Studies in British Art, which has close links with Yale University.

'Judge-Land'

THE PEAK OF THE PROFESSION

Bloomsbury's proximity to the Inns of Court made it
a favoured residence for leading members of the
legal profession throughout the eighteenth and nineteenth centuries, so much so that it won the nickname 'Judge-Land'.

The great William Murray, Earl of Mansfield
(1705-93), whose fine house and precious library at 28-9 Bloomsbury Square were sacked
and burned by anti-Catholic rioters in 1780, conducted the trial of their leader, the half-mad Lord
George Gordon, so impartially that he was acquitted.
The poet William Cowper was so incensed by the
outrage committed upon the learned judge that he
composed an entire poem *On the Burning of Lord
Mansfield's Library Together with his MSS by the Mob
in the Month of June 1780.* When Boswell, defending
his countrymen from one of Johnson's habitual jibes
at Scotsmen, invoked the career of Mansfield, Solicitor-General at the age of 37, as a counter-argument,
the old bear would have none of it, pointing out that
he had been educated at Westminster and "Much

*75. William Murray, Lord Mansfield, from the painting by Sir
Joshua Reynolds.*

*74. Troops encamped in the grounds of the British Museum
during the Gordon Riots of 1780.*

76. *Lord Eldon*

77. *Lord Thurlow*

may be made of a Scotchman, if he be caught young." Mansfield was commemorated by his contemporaries with a huge memorial in Westminster Abbey - against his express wishes. Civil rights campaigners remember him for his ruling in the case of James Somersett, a black slave whom his owner wished to repatriate to the colonies by force. Mansfield decreed this illegal, thus greatly encouraging the anti-slavery movement, though, scrupulous of property rights, he attacked neither slavery nor the slave-trade as such. Indeed, lawyers remember him as the founding father of commercial law, thanks to his efforts to enlarge notions of property and contract to embrace trade as comprehensively as agriculture.

Mansfield's near-contemporary, Lord Thurlow (1731-1806), was likewise Solicitor-General before the age of forty. Violently opposed to both the anti-slavery movement and the grievances of the American colonies, he had an especial dislike of the radical defender of these causes, Charles James Fox (1749-1806), whose be-toga'd statue (anachronistically clutching the scroll of Magna Carta) now stands in Bloomsbury Square. Ugly and overbearing, Thurlow, according to Fox, nevertheless 'looked wiser than any man ever *was*.' The arch-reactionary suffered the profound irritation of having the Great Seal of England stolen from his home at 45 Great Ormond Street. It was never recovered, presumably because it was

simply melted down for its silver.

Lord Eldon (1751-1838) who lived at 42 Gower Street from 1791 to 1804 and then occupied 6 Bedford Square from 1804 to 1815, shared Thurlow's outlook, vehemently opposing the emancipation of slaves abroad and of Catholics at home. He served as Lord Chancellor almost continuously from 1801 to 1827 and in 1815 played a leading part in the passage of the Corn Laws, a tariff structure which protected English landowners from cheap imports of grain at the expense of the poor. An enraged mob gathered outside his residence and began to smash the windows. Unlike Mansfield, who prudently ducked out the back of his house in similar circumstances, the dour Geordie judge stood defiantly in the doorway, levelling a shotgun at his besiegers. Lady Eldon, meanwhile, did dash out the back, summoning guards picketed in the gardens of the British Museum. Led by a quick-witted corporal, they gave the impression of being an overwhelming force and dispersed the rioters but Eldon still vacated his official residence shortly afterwards. A wit of the day, punning on the smashed windows and the Lord Chancellor's notorious thriftiness, observed that this was a pity as he had been 'glad to note Lord Eldon had at last begun to keep an open house.' The following year, 1816, Eldon, thoroughly confirmed in his hatred for radicals of every type, denied Shelley custody of his two chil-

dren after the death of their mother, on the grounds
of the poet's atheism. Sydney Smith observed that
"Lord Eldon and the Court of Chancery sat heavy on
mankind". Eldon's one progressive contribution to
the legal system was the vigorous protection of trade-
marks by mercilessly hounding their abusers.

Eldon's contemporary, Sir Samuel Romilly (1757-
1818), was no less stout-hearted than the Lord Chancellor but quite the opposite in his outlook. As a
Gray's Inn man he had rushed to join its defenders
during the riots of 1780 but as Solicitor-General from
1806 onwards he worked tirelessly to reform the
cruelties and absurdities of the criminal code, miti-
gating over-harsh sentences and drastically reducing
the number of offences which then carried a manda-
tory death penalty - such as mugging. A disciple of
Bentham, he also supported the anti-slavery movement and the struggle for Catholic emancipation.
Successively an occupant of Gray's Inn and Gower
Street, he finally settled at 21 Russell Square where
his beloved wife died suddenly in 1818. Apparently
drawing little strength from his family motto - 'Per-
severe' - he cut his throat three days later.

Romilly's neighbour, Baron Denman (1779-1854),
who lived on the opposite side of the square, at No.
50, was also an anti-slaver. As Solicitor-General he
gallantly pleaded the cause of the luckless and ob-
noxious Queen Caroline before the House of Lords in
1820; but he also prosecuted the rioters on behalf of
parliamentary reform in 1832 and as Lord Chief
Justice condemned the publisher of Shelley's complete works for blasphemy.

Of Bloomsbury's other lawyers one has a minor
claim to fame as a literary foot-note. Theodore Watts-
Dunton (1832-1914), solicitor and groupie to the Pre-
Raphaelites, lived at 15 Great James Street from 1872-3
and 'rescued' the bohemian poet Algernon Swinburne
from a life of self-destructive debauchery. Swinburne
showed his gratitude by never writing anything of
note thereafter.

78. *Samuel Romilly*

Healers and Hospitals

THE CROWN'S CONSULTANTS

'Our part of London is so very superior to most others... The neighbourhood of Brunswick Square is very different from all the rest. We are so very airy.... Mr.Wingfield thinks the vicinity of Brunswick Square the most favourable as to air.'

The therapeutic reputation of Bloomsbury was firmly established long before Isabella, sister of Jane Austen's 'Emma', proclaimed its virtues so forthrightly - not least by having been the residence of no less than five royal physicians.

Dr Mead, physician to George II, lived and died (in 1754), at 49 Great Ormond Street where his salon attracted men of science and letters, drawn equally by his library of 10,000 volumes and a fine collection of antique treasures which realised £16,000 at his death. Bloomsbury Place was home from 1695 to 1742 to an even greater collector, Sir Hans Sloane, whose collection helped to found the British Museum.

Bloomsbury Square housed Sloane's predecessor, Dr Radcliffe, whose professional approach to royalty appears to have been decidedly off-hand. Having examined William III for gout he pronounced 'I would not have your Majesty's two legs for your three kingdoms.' His treatment of Queen Mary, who died of smallpox at the age of 32, was severely questioned, which perhaps explains why he flatly refused to attend her successor, Anne, as she lay dying - ironically pleading that he was too ill himself to come. Nevertheless he became rich enough to be one of Oxford University's greatest benefactors.

The same square was also home to Mark Akenside (1721-70), a consultant to George III's consort, Queen Charlotte. Akenside's humble origins (he was the son of a Newcastle butcher), coupled with his physical disability (he had one leg shorter than the other) led him to adopt a haughty manner, while his undoubted learning made him something of a pedant. Smollett, himself a doctor, satirised him in *Peregrine Pickle*. Akenside's long poem The *Pleasures of the Imagination* was, however, both admired and influential and he has subsequently been regarded as a fore-runner of the Romantics, though the posthumous publication of his collected verse prompted Johnson to observe that 'One bad Ode may be suffered, but a number of them together makes one sick.'

The fifth royal physician was Dr Willis, who attempted to cure the wretched George III of his recurrent bouts of madness. Willis had rooms in Queen Square and here, in a pathetic attempt to lure the

79. Dr Richard Mead; portrait by Allan Ramsay, 1747.

80. A portrait, thought to be of Dr John Radcliffe, by an unknown artist.

81. *The earlier University College Hospital building, seen across the road from University College.*

82. *Thomas Wakley, founder of* The Lancet.

demented monarch back to sanity, his wife, the devoted Charlotte, prepared his favourite dishes with her own hand, storing the ingredients in the rented cellar of a public house - now known as 'The Queen's Larder.' Perhaps the king would have been better off in the hands of William Battie, a resident of Great Russell Street and proprietor of a highly profitable lunatic asylum, who died worth £100,000.

SPECIALISTS AND PIONEERS

Around the royal physicians clustered a notable array of specialists. Quaker John Fothergill, an expert on sore throats, lived and died in Harpur Street. Sheldon, the anatomist, was to be found in Great Russell Street. Robert Willan (1757-1812), the first English physician to classify skin diseases, lived in Bloomsbury Square.

Bloomsbury was also home to the bizarre Martin van Butchell, who wore a waist-length beard, rode a pony painted purple with black spots and kept the embalmed corpse of his first wife in a glass-fronted box. Perhaps it was this sort of practitioner that Thomas Wakley (1795-1862) of 35 Bedford Square was out to expose when he founded *The Lancet* in 1823 to combat fraud in the medical profession.

Wakley's other major achievement was the passage of legislation in 1860 to combat the adulteration of food and drink.

The increasing professionalisation of medicine in Wakley's time is attested by a significant number of Bloomsbury residents and landmarks.

University College Hospital, which began as an out-patient dispensary at Euston Square in 1828, relocated to Gower Street in 1834 as the North London Hospital, assuming its present name in 1837. Joseph Lister, pioneer of antiseptic surgery, enrolled as a student here in 1844, having been barred from Oxbridge on account of his Quaker faith. In 1846 Robert Liston performed Europe's first operation under ether here, having recently witnessed this daring new procedure in Boston, Mass. Once the patient's leg had been safely amputated, Liston turned to his students and declared triumphantly "This Yankee dodge, gentlemen, beats mesmerism hollow!" The reference would not have been lost on his audience - the first Professor of Surgery at U.C.H. having been dismissed for experimenting with mesmerism (hypnosis) instead of relying on traditional opiates, such as laudanum.

Barely two hundred yards further down Gower Street was the residence of James Robinson (1813-62) who pioneered the application of anaesthetics in dentistry. Between the two, however, lay Keppel Street, where Dickens' father died - five years after Liston's demonstration - following an agonising operation to remove stones from his bladder, without the benefit of any anaesthetic.

Thomas Hodgkin (1798-1866), who first accurately described the glandular disorder which bears his name, succeeded Wakley at 35 Bedford Square. Hodgkin's neighbour at No. 3, Dr.Theophilus Thompson, built his career around the recommendation of cod liver oil as a sovereign remedy.

The polymath Dr Peter Mark Roget (1779-1869) lived in Gower Street and Great Russell Street before settling for thirty-five years at 39 Bernard Street. A member of the Geological Society, the Royal Astronomical Society, the Zoological Society, the Royal Geographical Society and the Royal Entomological Society, Roget was also a founder of the Athenaeum and the Society for the Diffusion of Useful Knowledge and Secretary of the Royal Society. He did not begin compiling the *Thesaurus* that bears his name until he was over 70.

The following generation of Bloomsbury practitioners included such notable pioneers as Sir Rickman Godlee, the first surgeon to remove a brain tumour, Sir Victor Horsley, the first to remove a spinal tumour and Sir Thomas Lewis, pioneer of electrocardiography. Sir Frederick Treves (1853-1923), who lived at 18 Gordon Square from 1880-84, developed a high-profile career as protector of the 'El-

83. Caricature by Thomas Rowlandson, 1783, of surgeons conducting an amputation without anaesthetic.

84. Joseph Lister (1827-1912), a student at the University College Hospital.

ephant Man' and as the surgeon who took out King Edward VII's appendix. During the Great War Treves was instrumental in founding the British Red Cross. Louisa Aldrich-Blake (1865-1925), whose double-sided bronze bust stands in Tavistock Square, made her name by becoming the first woman in Britain to gain the degree of Master of Surgery. She went on to become Dean of the London School of Medicine for Women and was also renowned for her skill at cricket - and boxing.

THE BLOOMSBURY DISPENSARY

In 1801 the Bloomsbury Dispensary for the Relief of the Sick Poor opened its doors at 62 Great Russell Street, having secured an eighty-year lease from its patron, the Duke of Bedford. Access to treatment depended on a patient bringing a letter of recommendation from a local clergyman or from one of the local residents whose contributions supported the institution. Almost a thousand patients were treated in the first year and this remained an average figure for the first decade. They came especially from the slum areas largely colonised by Irish immigrants, and the run-down mews properties of the Foundling estate. The medical staff of the dispensary identified the major causes of illness as inadequate diet, insanitary living conditions and unsafe working practices. Apart from consumption and typhoid, a large proportion of the most serious cases were the outcome of prostitution or industrial injuries, poisoning etc. sustained as a by-product of working in the back-street furniture and upholstery workshops which supplied the smart stores along Tottenham Court Road and Oxford Street. Epidemic outbreaks could lead to a suspension of the normal rules. During the cholera outbreak of 1849-50 so many were treated that the files failed to record them all: 'the doors of the Institution were kept open for several hours daily, the usual letter of recommendation being dispensed with.'

In terms of medical history the Dispensary's main claim to fame was the appointment of Dr.Edward Jenner (1749-1823) to the novel post of Superintendent of Vaccine Inoculation. In his native Gloucestershire Jenner, the founding father of immunology, had experimented with the use of 'cow-pox' to inoculate against small-pox for some years before publicly proclaiming its efficacy in 1798. In 1800 he came to London to establish a 'vaccine institution'. In the Bloomsbury dispensary he found one ready-made. Lodging at 15 Bedford Place, Jenner stayed for little more than a year, turning his back on the possibility of a brilliant metropolitan practice to return to his country home. Nevertheless he remained a member of the Dispensary's Medical Committee until his death and the programme of vaccination went steadily ahead after his departure. Over the course of a ten year period some 825 inoculations were carried out, including all the inmates of the Foundling Hospital - where smallpox was henceforth eliminated. A measure of the desperate conditions to be found on the fringes of elegant, respectable Bloomsbury, however, is the fact that a century after Jenner's pioneering campaign there were still six cases of smallpox treated by the Dispensary in a single year.

Just as the Dispensary's eighty-year lease ran out a timely legacy enabled it to acquire a new one and pay

85. *Edward Jenner; oil painting by James Northcote.*

for a new building as well. Numbered 22 Bloomsbury Street, it actually had most of its frontage facing onto Streatham Street. The new premises had the advantage of being not only purpose-built but much larger, which was no doubt much appreciated by the hard-pressed staff who were by now treating some 5,000 cases a year. The transition was supervised by the distinguished surgeon Henry Morris, who served the Dispensary for over fifty years, and whose eminence was recognised by a baronetcy and the Presidency of the Royal College of Surgeons.

During the inter-war period the Dispensary began to adjust to the fact that Bloomsbury was fast losing its permanent residential population and so offered a new service by providing pupils of local schools with treatment for minor accidents and ailments. The effective work of the Dispensary ended with its destruction by enemy bombs in November 1940 and April 1941, though its endowment enabled it to carry on making grants for charitable and medical purposes into the post-war period.

86. The Bloomsbury Dispensary in Bloomsbury Street.

87. *The new Hospital for Sick Children in Great Ormond Street; from* The Builder, *1872.*

SPECIALISED CENTRES

The second half of the nineteenth century witnessed the establishment of a clutch of specialised medical institutions virtually side by side. The Hospital for Sick Children opened in 1852 in the former home of Dr Mead in Great Ormond Street; purpose-built accommodation had to wait another twenty years. In 1856 the Roman Catholic Hospital of SS. John and Elizabeth was established in the same street by Cardinal Wiseman. In 1859 the London Homeopathic Hospital removed from Golden Square to the Queen Square corner of Great Ormond Street. In the following year the National Hospital for Nervous Diseases (originally the National Hospital for the Paralysed and Epileptics) admitted its first patients. It soon established itself as a world-class centre for the treatment of neurological diseases and could boast four Fellows of the Royal Society on its teaching staff. In 1866 a home for aged incurables was established in what had once been the Queen Square home of Edward Hoyle, the authority on card games. The following year saw the opening next door of the Alexandra Hospital for the treatment of poor children and, in Brunswick Row, of the Hospital for Hip Diseases in Childhood. In 1884 the *Ospedale Italiano* was established on the south side of Queen Square to cater to the long-established Italian communities of

88. *The Nurses' Home of the Hospital for Sick Children, c1926.*

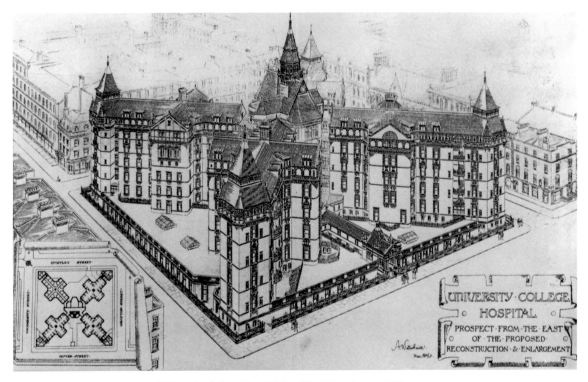

89. Plan for the reconstruction of University College Hospital, by Alfred Waterhouse, 1896.

90. The London Homeopathic Hospital, 1926.

neighbouring Clerkenwell and Soho. The present century has maintained something of this momentum with the rebuilding (1897-1906) of University College Hospital to the designs of Sir Alfred Waterhouse and the construction of the School of Hygiene and Tropical Medicine (1926-8) in Keppel Street, Lutyens' handsome headquarters for the British Medical Association (1922-9) on Tavistock Square, the somewhat less pleasing headquarters of the Pharmaceutical Society (1939) on Brunswick Square and the imposing library of the Wellcome Institute for the History of Medicine (1931) on the Euston Road.

In Dickens' Footsteps

DICKENS IN DOUGHTY STREET

When Charles Dickens (1812-70) married Catherine Hogarth they first set up home in his lodgings at Furnival's Inn. (The site is now covered by the Gothic headquarters of the Prudential Assurance Company on High Holborn.) The birth of a son necessitated their departure from what were essentially bachelor quarters and in March 1837 they moved to their first proper marital home, at No. 48 Doughty Street, the only one of Dickens' ten London addresses to survive to the present. It was then a private road, with gates and a porter in an imposing uniform. Assuming an annual rental of £80, the author was somewhat in awe of his 'frightfully first-class Family Mansion, involving awful responsibilities.' The twelve room house had four floors and Dickens found himself the employer of a cook, a housemaid, a nurse and eventually a manservant. He chose to have his study in a

first floor back room, overlooking the garden. The woodwork of the house was gaily painted in pink; bright, patterned carpets were strewn on the floors and mirrors were installed to increase the interior light. The window-boxes were planted with the author's favourite flowers, geraniums. Fussily neat in ordering his household as much as his appearance, Dickens arranged every piece of furniture just so.

Dickens' delight in his new home was almost immediately overshadowed by the sudden death of his sister-in-law Mary in May 1837. Just 17, she literally died in his arms. In his masterly biography Peter Ackroyd notes that:

'His grief was so intense... that it represented the most powerful sense of loss and pain he was ever to experience. The deaths of his own parents and children were not to affect him half so much...'.

Thereafter Dickens wore a ring from her finger, and kept not only a lock of her hair but all her clothes as well. For the first and last time in his life he missed writing deadlines. Ackroyd surmises that Mary Hogarth represented his idealised image of the female and notes that his epitaph for her - 'Young, beautiful and good' - were the very words he was to

91. Charles Dickens at about the time of his residence in Doughty Street. Portrait by Daniel Maclise.

92. Mary Hogarth, Dickens' sister-in-law, who died in Doughty Street in 1837. Portrait by Hablot Knight Browne.

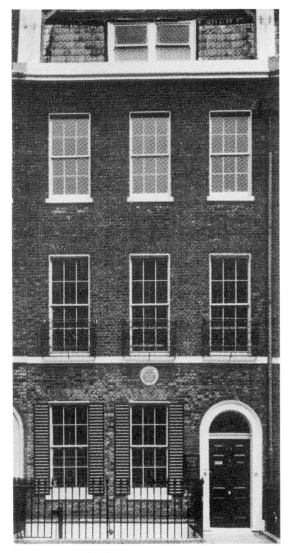

93. No. 48 Doughty Street

DICKENS IN TAVISTOCK HOUSE

Dickens moved back to Bloomsbury in 1851, taking up residence in Tavistock House, an eighteen-room mansion which was to be the last home he would share with his wife. Its extensive - and expensive - refurbishment included the construction of a small stage in a first floor back room. Dickens dubbed it 'The Smallest Theatre in the World' and used it to present the New Year shows in which he delighted. The author Wilkie Collins, Mark Lemon, the editor of *Punch* and the painter Augustus Egg were among his willing accomplices. Visitors to the house included Thackeray, Hans Christian Andersen, Harriet Beecher Stowe, Nathaniel Hawthorne and George Eliot, who wrote rather snidely of its 'splendid library... with soft carpet, couches etc., such as became a sympathiser with the suffering classes.' Luxury library notwithstanding, Tavistock House was not to provide a happy or even a particularly helpful setting for Dickens' writing and as he wrestled with the composition of *Bleak House* he began what would become a lifelong habit of providing himself with a bolt-hole to work in, renting rooms in remote suburban areas like New Cross and North Finchley. Despite the complications this arrangement necessarily involved Dickens not only managed to contribute prolifically to his weekly periodical *Household Words* but also to produce *Hard Times*, *Little Dorrit* and *A*

94. Private theatricals at Tavistock House

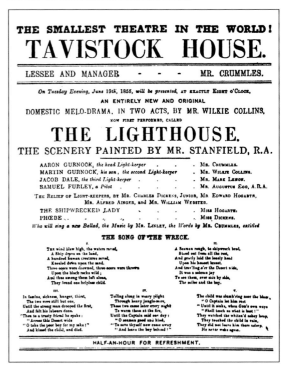

apply to such fictional creations as Little Nell and Florence Dombey.

It was at Doughty Street that Dickens completed *Pickwick Papers* and wrote both *Oliver Twist* and most of *Nicholas Nickleby* and began work on *Barnaby Rudge* and it was here that he celebrated his 27th birthday in the company of critic Leigh Hunt, fellow-novelist Harrison Ainsworth and his friend and biographer John Forster.

By the close of 1839 the further enlargement of the author's family prompted him to quit Doughty Street for a grander house at 1 Devonshire Terrace on the corner of Marylebone Road and Marylebone High Street.

95. The group of houses which contained Tavistock House

96. A Christening in Bloomsbury. Drawn by George Cruikshank for Sketches from Boz.

Tale of Two Cities. In 1858 Dickens finally parted from his wife. He stuck it out at Tavistock House until 1860, then sold up, moving to his Kentish home at Gad's Hill Place, near Rochester. He never had a permanent home in London again and, turning his back on the capital, he also tried to turn his back on the past, burning every letter he had received over twenty years, from Carlyle, Tennyson, Thackeray.......

BLOOMSBURY IN DICKENS

One of Dickens' earliest published pieces, written for *The Monthly Magazine* in 1832 and subsequently collected in *Sketches by Boz* is entitled *The Bloomsbury Christening*. The home of the family concerned, the Kitterbells, is located at 14 Great Russell Street (now a specialist film bookshop, but marked with a blue plaque) and the actual ceremony takes place in St George's, a couple of streets away.

Barnaby Rudge, written soon after Dickens left Doughty Street, is set against the background of the Gordon Riots of 1780, which the author researched meticulously. His descriptions of the mob violence are vivid and convincing and include an account of the sacking of Lord Mansfield's fine house in Bloomsbury Square.

Gray's Inn, where Dickens himself worked as a clerk and where Pickwick's solicitor Mr.Perker kept his offices, also provided lodgings for David Copperfield and Dora, in the house over the arch which marked its entrance, while Rosabud in *The Mystery of Edwin Drood* lodged with Miss Twinkleton at Mrs Billicken's house in Southampton Place.

A keen supporter of the Foundling Hospital, Dickens attended its Sunday chapel services quite regularly. Tattycoram - the name of the foundling in *Little Dorrit* confirms this sympathy.

In 1858 Dickens delivered what Ackroyd has called 'arguably his finest and most powerful address' - on behalf of the Hospital for Sick Children in Great Ormond Street. It had 31 beds - while 20,000 children died in the capital each year. Dickens' speech that night raised £3,000, securing the hospital on a sound financial footing for the first time. In *Our Mutual Friend* the waif Johnny finally dies in Great Ormond Street.

97. The cover for the instalments of The Mystery of Edwin Drood, *the last novel by Dickens.*

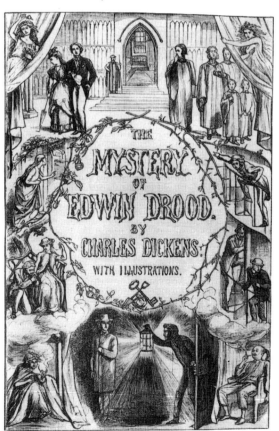

98. The final reading given by Dickens at St James's Hall, London, on 15 March, 1870, as depicted in the Illustrated London News. *The desk is now housed in the Dickens Museum.*

THE DICKENS MUSEUM

The Dickens Fellowship bought the Doughty Street house in 1924. Its contents include not only the world's most comprehensive library of Dickens criticism, but also his writing desk and some of the original playbills he had printed for his home theatricals. The basement has been furnished to represent the kitchen at Dingley Dell as described in the *Pickwick Papers*. Several of Dickens' autograph manuscripts are on display at the British Museum - where he himself often worked.

Rebels and Reformers

Bloomsbury's "birds of a feather" syndrome appears to have applied quite as much to philanthropists as it does to artists, architects, actors and authors. Perhaps the establishment of the Foundling Hospital provided a nucleus of concern.

Teetotal, vegetarian John Howard (1726-90) of 23 Great Ormond Street, made prison reform his special crusade, battling to stamp out corruption and impose basic standards of hygiene; ironically he died inspecting prisons in Russia while on a mission to find effective treatments for infectious diseases. Contemporaries were so impressed by Howard's selfless zeal that he was honoured with the first memorial to be erected in St.Paul's Cathedral. The Howard League for Penal Reform is so named in his honour.

TWO TRAGEDIES

No such honour marked the passing of Mary Wollstonecraft (1759-97), who lived in Store Street

99. John Howard

100. Mary Wollstonecraft; from the oil painting by John Opie

while writing a *Vindication of the Rights of Women*, arguably the primal text of feminist literature. The normally urbane, if waspish, Horace Walpole referred to her as 'a philosophizing serpent.... hyena in petticoats' and the *Historical Magazine* pronounced confidently, if ambiguously, that 'her works will be read with disgust by every female who has any pretensions to delicacy.' After an unhappy love affair with a feckless, philandering American, she attempted suicide (by jumping off Putney Bridge) and then took up with the radical William Godwin, then living in Gower Place. Against her principles she succumbed to convention by marrying Godwin once she became pregnant. She died within days of the birth of her daughter, Mary (1797-1881) who grew up to marry Shelley and write the original *Frankenstein*.

The *Monthly Visitor* no doubt thought it was having the last word when it pronounced smugly in an obituary of Mary Wollstonecraft that:

'In all probability had she been married well in early life, she had then been a happy woman and universally respected.'

Over a century later, Virginia Woolf passionately contradicted any such attempt to consign the pioneer feminist to oblivion:

'Many millions have died and been forgotten in the hundred and thirty years that have passed since she was buried: and yet as we read her letters and listen to her arguments and consider her experiments.... and realize the high-handed and hot-blooded

101. *Eleanor Marx*

102. *Robert Owen*

manner in which she cut her way to the quick of life, one form of immortality is hers undoubtedly: she is alive and active.... we hear her voice and trace her influence even now among the living.'

A parallel to the tragedy of Mary Wollstonecraft's life can be seen in that of Eleanor Marx (1855-98) who, from 1884 to 1890, likewise courted scandal by living openly at 55 Great Russell Street with her lover, Dr Edward Aveling. During this period she took a leading part in organizing the unprecedented, sensational and ultimately successful strike of the female labour force of Bryant & May's East End match factory. Unfortunately Eleanor never even found her Godwin. When she discovered that Aveling was already married to an actress she was completely shattered and committed suicide at 135 Gower Street by swallowing Prussic acid - which Aveling, a scientist, had obtained for her.

SECULARISTS AND CHRISTIANS
The turbulent decade of the 1830s, which saw the reform of Parliament, the creation of the University of London, ambitious and ill-fated experiments in trade unionism and the birth of the Chartist and Co-operative movements, was much influenced by three

reformers living within yards of each other in what was then Burton Crescent and is now Cartwright Gardens.

Robert Owen (1771-1858) lived at 4 Crescent Place. Under the influence of Bentham, he progressed from model factory-owner to utopian socialist visionary. Having recently experienced the failure of his project for a model community at New Harmony, Indiana, he turned to supervising a scheme for an Exchange Co-operative Bazaar which shared a former horse repository in the Gray's Inn Road with Madame Tussaud's Exhibition and Promenade before the latter's removal to Baker Street.

Major Cartwright (1740-1824), after whom this elegant area was re-named, was a professional serving officer who so far sympathised with America's revolutionaries that he refused to fight against them and even got up a fund to relieve the families of the rebels killed at Lexington and Concord. A doughty anti-slaver, he not only advocated universal suffrage but annually-elected parliaments as well. The third notable occupant of this still elegant area was Rowland Hill (1795-1879), a supporter of Owen, a founder of the Society for the Diffusion of Useful Knowledge and far-sighted inventor of the penny post.

103. The London Horse Repository in Gray's Inn Road, a building later used by Robert Owen for his Exchange Co-operative Bazaar.

104. Sir Rowland Hill

Whereas Owen, Cartwright and Hill were essentially belated children of the Enlightenment and primarily secular in their motivation, their counterparts in Russell Square were fervent Christians, albeit of the combative variety.

F.D. Maurice (1805-72) was the founder of Christian Socialism and the Working Men's College as its practical expression. Appointments at Guy's Hospital and Lincoln's Inn brought a wide circle of professional young men under his influence. With their keen assistance he set about redirecting the energies of the discontented from Chartism to self-improvement. From 1846 to 1856 he lived in 'quiet and antiquated' Queen Square, then moved to a much larger house at 5 Russell Square, where the Hotel Russell now stands. Maurice's daily routine began with a cold bath at 6 a.m., followed by a no doubt brisk and glowing walk over to King's College, where he was Professor of English Literature and History until he was dismissed for his unorthodox refusal to believe in hell-fire and damnation.

Sir George Williams (1821-1905) certainly did believe in hell-fire and damnation, coupled with the firm conviction that the most certain way to get there was to imbibe the demon drink. As President of the Band of Hope he thundered from pulpits at the impressionable young but he is chiefly remembered

105. *Mary Augusta (Mrs Humphry) Ward.*

for his more enduring contribution as founder of the YMCA.

Mrs Humphry Ward (1851-1920) moved into 61 Russell Square when her husband joined *The Times* in 1881. Her novel *Robert Elsmere*, published in 1888, caused a sensation by asserting the primacy of the social gospel over evangelising in Christianity's order of priorities. A hyper-active supporter of good causes and a prolific novelist, Mrs. Ward was also violently opposed to votes for women and served as President of the Anti-Suffrage League. She is memorialised by the Mary Ward Centre in Tavistock Place. Built in 1897-8 to the Arts & Crafts designs of Smith and Brewer, two very young University of London men, it is praised unreservedly by Pevsner as 'one of the most charming pieces of architecture designed at that time in England'.

The Mary Ward Centre was originally named in honour of her collaborator, the open-handed John Passmore Edwards (1823-1911), who lived at 51 Bedford Square. Originally a Chartist and an outspoken opponent of the death penalty, corporal punishment, the Crimean war and the Boer war, he made a fortune out of publishing and spent most of it founding twenty-four free libraries as well as funding a multiplicity of other public facilities from hospitals to horse-troughs. He declined a knighthood from both Queen Victoria and Edward VII.

CHARITIES

Apart from these worthy individuals Victorian Bloomsbury was also home to a dozen or more charitable institutions. In Bloomsbury Square were the offices of the Royal Literary Fund (to sub impoverished authors) and the National Benevolent Institution, while adjoining Bloomsbury Place accommodated the Corporation of the Sons of the Clergy (to sub the offspring of impoverished priests). In Queen Square there were two Roman Catholic charities - the Aged Poor Society and the Society of Vincent de Paul, with the UK Benefit Society in adjoining Great Ormond Street. New Ormond Street housed the headquarters of the Workhouse Visiting Society and Regent Square the Home of Hope 'for the reception of such young women.... as are unfitted, from their previous character and position, for the general wards of a workhouse.'

Bloomsbury maintains to this day a strong presence of charitable institutions, having the offices of the Royal National Institute for the Deaf, the National Council for Voluntary Service, the National Institute of Social Work, the Central Council for Education and Training in Social Work and the Social Work branch of the Salvation Army.

FAITHFULL FORERUNNER

Bloomsbury could fairly claim to be the forcing-house of the movement for women's suffrage. But forty years before the suffrage issue came to dominate British politics Bloomsbury had housed a notable experiment in female self-emancipation. Emily Faithfull's skilfully-named Victoria Press was established in Great Coram Street in 1860, with the express approval of Queen Victoria herself, to provide employment for an all-female staff of compositors and printers. Emily Faithfull (1835-1894), novelist, essayist and publicist for the feminist cause, was one of the founding members of the Society for Promoting the Employment of Women. Printing was considered a suitable trade for women because it required 'chiefly a quick eye, a ready hand and steady application' but involved 'no exposure to weather, no hard labour'. The main product of the Victoria Press was *The English Woman's Journal* (1858-64), a pioneering publication for the feminist cause, but within a year of its establishment, having expanded its work-force from five to sixteen, it was also publishing a weekly newspaper *The Friend of the People*, a legal quarterly and numerous sermons and pamphlets. In 1863 Emily Faithfull started up *The Victoria Magazine* but was obliged to dissociate herself from the Press in 1867 after she had been cited in a highly publicised divorce case and suspected of lesbianism. She continued, however, to be active in trade unionism and the printing trade and in 1877 founded the *West London Express*.

106. Emily Faithfull

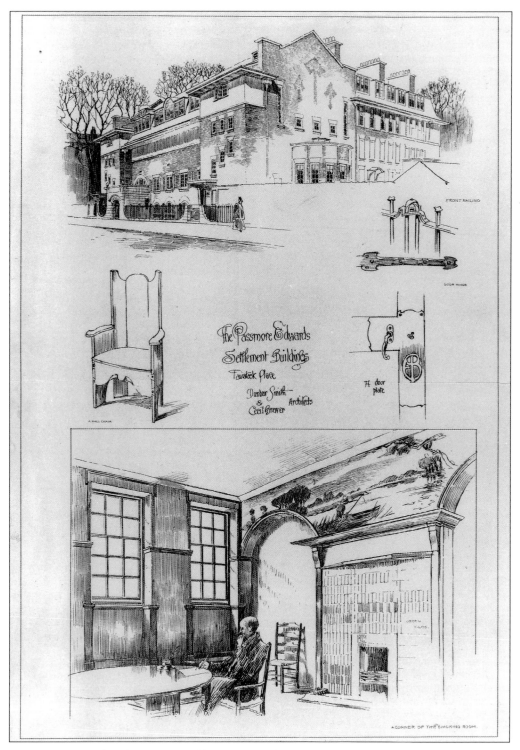

107. *The Passmore Edwards Settlement Buildings in Tavistock Place - later called the Mary Ward Centre.*

SUFFRAGISTS AND SUFFRAGETTES

In 1909 the then Passmore Edwards Settlement staged a public debate between Mary Ward and Millicent Garrett Fawcett (1849-1929) on the issue of votes for women. Mrs Ward lost by 235 votes to 74 and vowed backstage to her opponent 'I shall never do this sort of thing again, never.' Mrs. Fawcett lived at 2 Gower Street with her husband Henry (1833-84) who, although blinded in a shooting accident, had become a good skater and card-player, a professor at Cambridge, a Member of Parliament and, as Postmaster General, invented postal orders, parcel post, savings stamps and the pillar-box plaque that advises the number of the next collection. By the time Mrs. Emmeline Pankhurst (1858-1928) founded her Women's Social and Political Union in 1903 Millicent Fawcett had been campaigning for the women's vote for over thirty years. In 1908 she was serving as president of the National Union of Women's Suffrage Societies when it broke with the WSPU over the issue of violence. Mrs. Fawcett, dismissed by Sylvia Pankhurst as 'a trim, prim little figure with a clear, pleasant voice', actually defended the militant wing of the movement against its critics in her memoirs but held firmly to her own conviction that :

'I can never feel that setting fire to houses and churches and letter-boxes and destroying valuable

108. Christabel Pankhurst.

pictures really helps to convince people that women ought to be enfranchised.'

Mrs Pankhurst, by contrast, proclaimed in 1912 that 'the argument of the broken pane of glass is the most valuable argument in modern politics.' The following year, however, saw a temporary truce between the various wings of the movement when they came together at a service in St George's Bloomsbury to honour the spectacular death of Emily Wilding Davison (1872-1913), who on Derby Day had swathed herself in the purple, white and green colours of the suffragettes and charged into the path of the king's horse. A convicted arsonist who had already thrown herself down a flight of prison steps to protest against the treatment of fellow prisoners, she almost certainly intended publicity rather than suicide, but died within hours as a result of her injuries.

Underlying differences about tactics were divergences in philosophy.

Millicent Fawcett saw the struggle for the vote as one strand of a battle on four fronts which also embraced educational and occupational opportunities and 'an equal moral standard between men and women.'

Mrs Pankhurst's daughter, Christabel (1880-1958), who had played in Russell Square as a child when the family was living at No.8, was perceived by her comrade Emmeline Pethwick-Lawrence as embodying an entirely new kind of womanhood:

'Christabel cared less for the political vote itself than for the dignity of her sex...to her the means were even more important than the end. Militancy to her meant the putting off of the slave spirit.'

A less publicly-acknowledged reason for the split between law-abiding suffragists and law-breaking suffragettes was the antagonism aroused by the autocratic style of the Pankhursts. A more democratically organised alternative to the WSPU had been founded in Barter Street the previous year; it pointedly adopted the name of Women's Freedom League.

Bloomsbury's further suffragette connections include the offices of the Men's League for Women's Suffrage, at 40 Museum Street, and the International Franchise Club at 66 Russell Square, which may well have inspired the Russell Square location of the fictional suffrage headquarters where volunteer campaigner Mary Datchett works tirelessly for the cause in Virginia Woolf's *Night and Day*. Gordon Square was the home of Lady Jane Strachey (1840-1928), suffragette and mother of Lytton, and mother-in-law of Ray Strachey (1887-1940), who also lived in Gordon Square and wrote the history of the suffrage movement under the title of *The Cause*, which was published in 1928, the year when women finally got the vote on the same terms as men.

Artists and Architects

PAST MASTERS

Bloomsbury's painterly tradition begins auspiciously with the residence in Great Russell Street of newly-arrived, German-born Gottfried Kniller (1646-1723) - who went on to paint ten reigning sovereigns, become rich and die Sir Godfey Kneller, being laid to rest in Westminster Abbey, with a fulsome epitaph by Pope. The outrageously vain Kneller only wanted a memorial, not a tomb, on the grounds that 'they do bury fools there'; Pope thought the epitaph 'the worst thing I ever wrote in my life.'

Kneller soon quit Great Russell Street for the more fashionable environs of Covent Garden, but his student, George Vertue (1684-1756), settled in Museum Street and produced more than five hundred engravings in the course of his career, as well as collecting notes for a projected art history of England, which eventually became the chief source material for Horace Walpole's *Anecdotes of Painting in England*.

Newly-wed John Constable (1776-1837) lived in Keppel Street from 1817 to 1822, during which time

110.   John Constable

111.   The right-hand house, No. 8 Keppel Street, was Constable's home from 1817 to 1822.

109.   Sir Godfrey Kneller; self-portrait, 1685

he was at last admitted to the Royal Academy. Constable's far more career-minded contemporary, fashionable portraitist Sir Thomas Lawrence (1769-1830), was admitted to the Royal Academy when he was just 21, half Constable's age at admission. He made his reputation in 1801 with a portrait of J.P. Kemble as Hamlet, which now hangs in the Tate Gallery. Lawrence became the third President of the Royal Academy in 1820, the year in which Constable exhibited *The Hay Wain*, and while he was completing his portraits of the statesmen and generals who defeated Napoleon, which now hang in the Waterloo Chamber of Windsor Castle. When the Russian general Platoff sat for Lawrence the doors of his Russell Square house were guarded by Cossacks on white chargers; the Imperial Hotel now stands on its site. Reviewing the works of Constable and Lawrence for *Le Journal de Paris* at the Salon of 1824, Stendhal thought the former 'truthful as a mirror' but confessed to puzzlement at Lawrence's standing:

'I do not understand the reputation of this painter... Mr Lawrence must be very clever or else our neighbours in London must be very poor connoisseurs.'

Lawrence was certainly a gifted draughtsman, having had his own studio from the age of twelve, and he had a 'pleasing manner' that served him well in society; gossipy Benjamin Haydon opined that 'he had smiled so long and so often that at last his smile wore the appearance of being set in enamel.' A

century later Bloomsbury art critic Roger Fry was to dismiss his talent as misplaced - 'the vision that Lawrence grasped so surely was relatively commonplace and undistinguished.'

COMMERCIAL SUCCESSORS

While Constable and Lawrence vied for the approval of public and posterity, their would-be successors took instruction at Sass's Drawing Academy at the southern end of Bloomsbury Street. Graduates of this establishment included John Millais (1829-96) and W.P. Frith (1819-1909), both of whom were to enjoy huge commercial success.

Millais, who lived at 7 Gower Street as a boy and at 83 as a young man, eventually achieved a knighthood and Presidency of the R.A. He first won notoriety with his painstakingly-detailed and self-consciously symbolic painting of *Christ in the House of his Parents*. Dickens, writing in *Household Words*, splutteringly denounced it as 'mean, odious, revolting and repulsive', describing the central figure as 'a hideous, wry-necked, blubbering red-headed boy in a nightgown' and the Virgin as 'so horrible in her ugliness that she would stand out from the rest of the company as a monster... in the lowest gin-shop in Europe.' Ruskin, the leading art critic of the day, sprang to the defence of Millais and his comrades. Millais expressed his gratitude in a letter which prompted Ruskin to visit him in Gower Street, acc-

112. Sir Thomas Lawrence

113. Sir John Millais

114. *Edward Burne-Jones*

115. *John Leech*

companied by his wife Effie - despite the fact that he thought the thoroughfare 'the *ne plus ultra* of ugliness in street architecture.' In due course all three went off on holiday together, as a result of which Millais further expressed his gratitude to his saviour by taking Effie off his hands.

Frith, who lived in Bloomsbury Street, is best remembered for crowded set-piece *tours-de-force* such as *Derby Day* (National Gallery). The Oxford Companion to Art summarises his career with a squelch: 'Trivial in artistic imagination, he recorded pullulating scenes from Victorian middle-class life.... with accurate verve and technical dexterity.' But he made a great deal of money doing it.

Sass's Drawing Academy was satirised by Thackeray as 'Gandish's' in *The Newcomes*.

Thackeray's neighbour in Great Coram Street, the caricaturist John Leech (1817-64), later moved to 9 Powis Place, Great Ormond Street and from 1854 to 1862 lived at 32 Brunswick Square. It is said that the great sculptor Flaxman saw Leech drawing as an infant of three and instantly recognised his outstanding talent. From 1841 onwards Leech was one of the leading artists for *Punch*, contributing over 3,000 pictures. He also supplied illustrations for the hugely popular Christmas Books produced by Dickens, who said they were 'always the drawings of a gentleman.'

THE PRB

Dante Gabriel Rossetti (1828-82), son of the Professor of Italian at King's College, was taught drawing by the Norwich artist Cotman, Professor of Drawing at King's College, and was also enrolled in a Bloomsbury drawing academy run by the son of the Rev. Thomas Cary, who was known to his father as a translator of Dante. In 1848 Rossetti joined with Millais and five other youths to form the Pre-Raphaelite Brotherhood. As the son of an ex-revolutionary immigrant, Rossetti imparted to it the melodramatic aura of a secret society but its purpose was to encourage the rejection of the prevailing academic taste in painting in favour of the alleged sincerity and freshness of the Middle Ages. Members signalled their allegiance to the cause by ostentatiously signing their paintings with the enigmatic initials PRB.

The members of the group drifted apart after about five years and Rossetti next cast his spell over William Morris (1834-96) and Edward Burne-Jones (1833-98), who took over occupation of his former apartments at 17 Red Lion Square. Morris quit studying architecture under G.E. Street and turned his hand to making furniture, while Burne-Jones devoted himself to painting the sort of medieval and mythical subjects favoured by Rossetti, only rather better. In 1861 the three joined together as 'The Firm' to produce high-quality furniture and fittings by traditional craft methods. Initially it had its premises at 8 Red Lion

116. Dante Gabriel Rossetti; self-portrait, 1846.

117. A Randolph Caldecott drawing for the John Gilpin story.

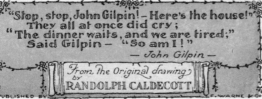

Square and from 1865 at 24 Queen Square. (Its presence and ideals are in a sense memorialised by the Art Workers' Guild currently based at 6 Queen Square.)

Burne-Jones produced many designs for stained-glass manufactured by The Firm as well as an altar-piece for Christ Church, Woburn Square in memory of Christina Rossetti (1830-94), poet and sister of Dante Gabriel, who lived at 30 Torrington Square from 1876 until her death.

Morris, apart from becoming a pioneer leader of the socialist movement, Professor of Poetry at Oxford and reviver of the art of fine book-production, took the lead in founding one of the earliest (1877) conservation bodies, the Society for the Protection of Ancient Buildings, which established its offices at Nos. 55-57 Great Ormond Street.

While Rossetti mourned the death of his wife and former model by consoling himself with Morris's wife and former model, reluctant bank-clerk Randolph Caldecott (1846-86) settled at 46 Great Russell Street and proceeded to establish himself as a brilliant illustrator of children's books, notably an edition of *John Gilpin*. A bout of rheumatic fever induced him to seek relief in the warmth of Florida - where he found an early grave.

118. William Morris

William Morris
Drawn by C. Fairfax Murray from a photograph. c 1870

119. *A picnic of Slade students c1912. In the back row David Bomberg is fourth from the right; Isaac Rosenberg is kneeling in the second row, and in the front row Dora Carrington is on the left, C.R.W. Nevinson third from left, Mark Gertler fourth from left; fourth from right is William Roberts and Stanley Spencer is second from right.*

TEACHING AND RESEARCH

The Slade School of Fine Art was established in University College in 1871 with water-colourist Sir Edward Poynter as its first Professor. He had already abandoned 106 Gower Street for a more fashionable address, Albert Gate. An able teacher and administrator, Poynter soon moved on to become Art Director at South Kensington and then Director of the National Gallery and finally to succeed Millais as President of the Royal Academy. Famous students of the Slade include W.R. Sickert, William Rothenstein, Augustus John, William Orpen, Wyndham Lewis and Stanley Spencer. Celebrated members of staff include William Coldstream, Roger Fry and Ernst Gombrich.

The Warburg Institute, established in Hamburg in 1866 for the study of the classical tradition and its impact on the arts, transferred to London after the Nazis' rise to power and was incorporated into the University in 1944, finding a temporary home at No. 1 Gordon Square, former residence of Charles Fowler (1791-1867), the architect of Covent Garden market. It moved into its Woburn Square home in 1958, sharing the building designed by Charles Holden, architect of Senate House, with the Courtauld Institute Galleries, which housed a world-class collection of Old Masters and Impressionists until they were transferred to Somerset House.

ECLECTIC AND GOTHIC

George Dance the Younger (1741-1825) was Surveyor to the City of London from 1768 to 1816 and one of the original forty Royal Academicians. Appointed Professor of Architecture, he appears never to have given a single lecture, although he did teach (Sir) John Soane, who was to prove a more brilliant architect than his mentor. Although much of Dance's work was inevitably done in the City itself, he did lay out Alfred Place, which belonged to the City Corporation and lies just west of his own house at 91 Gower Street. He was also a member of the committee which supervised the building of the Foundling Estate.

Dance was competent in a range of styles, from the brutal neo-Classicism of his lowering Newgate Prison to the whimsical Gothic-Oriental of the ceremonial entrance he devised for Guildhall. To Augustus Welby Pugin (1812-52) such eclecticism would have seemed positively unprincipled. The son of a French architect who settled at (now) 106 Great Russell Street and was employed by Nash, Pugin junior served his apprenticeship designing Kensal Green cemetery, scenery for Drury Lane theatre and furniture for Windsor Castle. In the course of a short and stormy life he was to be married three times, go bankrupt and pay off all his debts and die exhausted and half-mad from overwork. Cardinal Newman said of Pugin 'he has the great fault of a man of genius... He is intolerant and... sees nothing good in any school of

128. *George du Maurier.*

130. *Joseph Conrad with friend, Ellen Glasgow, in 1910.*

129. *Arthur Conan Doyle and his wife outside their home in South Norwood.*

Zenda (1894) in just a month. Its instant success enabled him to devote himself full-time to writing and come up with the equally rewarding *Rupert of Hentzau* in 1898. He was knighted for his services to the propaganda offensive during the Great War.

Jerome K. Jerome (1859-1927), who lived at 29 Queen Square, is chiefly remembered as the author of *Three Men in a Boat* (1889) - which sold a million copies in the United States alone; as these were pirated the author received not a penny piece in royalties. A Euston railway clerk turned actor, Jerome went on to co-edit *The Idler*, a humorous magazine, to write plays and to drive an ambulance in the Great War at the age of 55.

BLOOMSBURY SATELLITES

D.H. Lawrence (1885-1930) and his wife Frieda stayed at 44 Mecklenburgh Square for two months in 1917, having been more or less expelled from Cornwall on account of his outspoken pacifism and his wife's German connections. (She was a von Richthofen and a cousin of the 'Red Baron'). Lawrence was no stranger to the area, having been a regular correspondent of Lady Ottoline Morrell, whom he made the model for the eccentric Hermione Roddice in *Women in Love*. Lady Ottoline took such violent

131. *A letter from Anthony Hope-Hawkins to an admirer who liked 'Rudolf', dated 19 April 1903.*

132. *D.H. Lawrence.*

133. *Aldous Huxley.*

offence at this all-too-transparent representation of her that the insistent intervention of several friends was required to dissuade her from a libel suit.

The Lawrences' hostess on this occasion was the American, Dorothy Yorke, mistress of novelist Richard Aldington (1892-1962), who was serving in the army while his wife, the American Imagist poet, Hilda Doolittle (1886-1961), lived in another part of the same house, recovering from a miscarriage. Aldington, who was subsequently to leave his wife for his mistress, abruptly turned up on leave and soon after his reappearance the Lawrences moved out. D.H. Lawrence returned to Bloomsbury in 1925 during his last visit to England, and 'touched down for a few days' at 73 Gower Street.

After the war Dorothy L. Sayers (1893-1957) also came to live at 44 Mecklenburgh Square. Hard-pressed financially she sought salvation in the invention of a debonair sleuth, Lord Peter Wimsey. The success of her polished crime stories enabled her to move to 24 Great James Street in 1921 and use it as her London home for more than twenty years. *Murder Must Advertise* drew on her experiences of working in Benson's Advertising Agency in Holborn as a copy-writer.

Aldous Huxley (1894-1963), a descendant of Mrs Humphry Ward, lived briefly in Regent Square in

134. *George Orwell.*

135. *Lady Ottoline Morrell.*

1921, the year in which he published *Crome Yellow*, a country-house satire in which Lady Ottoline once again figured as a dottily absurd hostess. Many years later Lady Ottoline's erstwhile lover, Bertrand Russell, was to revenge the insult by dismissing Huxley's intellectual flashiness with the crushing observation that 'You could always tell by his conversation which volume of the *Encyclopaedia Britannica* he'd been reading. One day it would be Alps, Andes and Apennines and the next it would be Himalayas and the Hippocratic Oath.'

Thomas Burke (1886-1945), novelist of the East End, distanced himself safely from his subject-matter by living at 33 Tavistock Square in the 1930s. In 1939 he published a chatty account of *Living in Bloomsbury* and promptly moved to Queensway.

ORWELL

George Orwell (1903-50), like many other employees of the war-time BBC, became all too familiar with the Stalinesque corridors of Senate House while it functioned as the home of the Ministry of Information and revenged himself by making it the model for the Ministry of Truth in *1984*. This terrifying totalitarian nightmare confirmed the success he had won with *Animal Farm*; but his perverse decision to complete the manuscript on the bleak island of Jura finally undermined his precarious health. On September 3, 1949 he entered University College Hospital with the intention of restoring himself sufficiently to fly to Switzerland to make a full recovery. Freed from money worries at last, he took a private room at £17 a week - about the same as a month's wages for a working man. On October 13 Orwell, still confined to his sick-bed, married Sonia Brownell, the pretty secretary of Cyril Connolly, literary aesthete and school chum from Eton days. A reception was held at the Ritz in his absence. On 18 January 1950 Orwell made a new will in favour of the new Mrs.Orwell - and died three days later while his wife was out on a dinner-date.

Poets

LODGERS AND HOSTS

The pleasant setting of Russell Square appears to have attracted poets half a century before the square itself came into existence. William Cowper (1731-1800) and Thomas Gray (1716-71) both took lodgings at adjoining houses where the Imperial Hotel now stands, Gray praising the location for its 'air and sunshine and quiet'.

Cowper, a chronic depressive, is ironically best remembered for his comical account of the efforts of John Gilpin, 'a linen-draper bold' of Cheapside, to control a bolting horse when his intended canter into the countryside goes disastrously wrong - an intriguing demonstration of Cowper's own hymnal contention that 'God moves in a mysterious way'. Cowper's letters were much admired but Hazlitt noted perceptively a persistently timorous undertone to his work: 'He shakes hands with nature with a pair of fashionable gloves on.' Cowper's own gloomy verdict on himself was that 'I have no more right to the name of poet than a maker of mousetraps has to that of an engineer.'

Gray's *Elegy in a Country Churchyard* had already made him famous by the time he came to pursue his

137. *Thomas Gray; portrait by John Giles Eckhardt*

136. *William Cowper; engraving by Blake after Lawrence.*

antiquarian interests in the newly-founded British Museum in 1759. That very same year General James Wolfe, campaigning in Canada, announced to his no doubt startled comrades in arms, 'I would rather have written that poem, gentlemen, than take Quebec.' The very next day he took Quebec and fell in the hour of his victory. Johnson, with typical bluntness, still dismissed Gray's compositions as those of 'a mechanical poet' and explained his popularity as the result of being 'dull in a new way.'

Few poets could make a greater contrast to the retiring personalities of Cowper and Gray than Shelley (1792-1822), who lodged at 101 Great Russell Street and 19 Mabledon Place in 1816-17 while he vainly sought to gain custody of his children and made a fresh start with Mary Godwin when he could not. The sight of the massive statue of Rameses II in the British Museum inspired his best short poem, *Ozymandias*.

Few now recall the name of 'Barry Cornwall' - pseudonym (and deeply flawed anagram) of Brian Waller Procter (1787-1874), who lived briefly in Brunswick Square, at 25 Bedford Square (1825-32) and later in Southampton Row. A solicitor and barrister, he enjoyed popular success as a poet and lyricist. His daughter Adelaide contributed regularly to *Household Words*, edited by his friend Dickens. Mary Russell Mitford (1785-1855), flushed with the success of *Our*

138. Percy Bysshe Shelley; painting by George Clint.

140. Edward Fitzgerald; pencil drawing by Spedding.

139. Brian Waller Procter ('Barry Cornwall').

Village, stayed at 36 Russell Square in 1836 and met the gregarious Procter at a poet-packed dinner party, though he seems to have been recalled as something of an afterthought:

'Mr.Wordsworth, Mr.Landor and Mr.White dined here. I like Mr.Wordsworth.... Mr.Landor is a very striking-looking person, and exceedingly clever. Also we had a Mr Browning, a young poet, and Mr Procter, and Mr.Morley and quantities more of poets.'

Russell Square was also the boyhood home of Edgar Allan Poe (1809-49), and provided lodgings for Ralph Waldo Emerson (1803-82) when he first visited England in 1833.

Edward Fitzgerald (1809-83) is frequently credited with being the author of *The Rubaiyat of Omar Khayyam* and his translation of the Persian original is so free that he might as well have been. A highly accomplished linguist, he also translated Calderon and Sophocles. Friendly but reclusive, he lived most of his life in Suffolk but made frequent forays to London, sharing Thackeray's house in 1843 and settling at 19 Bedford Square from 1844-48.

Fitzgerald's amiable manner stands in sharp contrast to the tortured persona of Arthur Hugh Clough (1819-61), a star pupil of the charismatic Thomas

141. *Algernon Swinburne; caricature by 'Ape' for* Vanity Fair, *21 November 1874.*

Arnold at Rugby and youthful principal of University Hall. He considered his career a failure and was tortured by 'doubts'. His early death prompted paeans of praise and regret from such commanding Establishment figures as Bagehot, Jowett, Florence Nightingale and Dean Stanley. James Russell Lowell opined that he would 'be thought a hundred years hence to have been the truest expression in verse of... the doubt and struggle towards settled convictions, of the period in which he lived.' Matthew Arnold (whose *Dover Beach* far more adequately fulfills Lowell's prophecy) composed *Thyrsis* as a tribute to Clough but Swinburne anticipated the demolition job which Lytton Strachey was to execute in *Eminent Victorians:*

'There was a poor poet called Clough,
Whom his friends all united to puff,
    But the public, though dull,
      Had not such a skull
As belonged to believers in Clough.'

TWO ETONIANS

Swinburne (1837-1909), who lived variously in North Crescent, Upper Woburn Place, Great James Street and Guilford Street, was probably untroubled by such playful spite towards the memory of a singularly high-minded soul, having acquired from Eton a lasting taste for flagellation. He knew Rossetti and the Pre-Raphaelites and won early praise from Tennyson for his technical skill before his eroticism and rejection of Christianity brought down a torrent of abuse upon him. *Punch* suggested that he was really called Swine-born. The poet responded by stepping up his intake of drink and debauchery, which set him on a tread-mill of booze and blackmail until he was spirited away by Watts-Dunton to the less tempting climes of Putney and rationed to a lunch-time light ale. This restored his health but undermined his undoubted talents. Oscar Wilde observed that 'Watts is a solicitor and the business of a solicitor is to conceal crime. Swinburne's genius has been killed and Watts is doing his best to conceal it.'

Both Robert Browning and T.S. Eliot deplored Swinburne's verse and, even more, its influence but neither could match Carlyle's venomous description of the poet as a man standing up to his neck in a cesspool and adding to its contents.

Even as Swinburne quitted Bloomsbury, Robert Bridges (1844-1930), a fellow product of Eton and Oxford, moved in, sharing 52 Bedford Square with his mother and working a few minutes walk away at the Great Ormond Street Hospital for Sick Children. Bridges' Oxford friend, Gerard Manley Hopkins, was a frequent visitor during these years (1877-81) which also inspired Bridges' poems *London Snow* and *On a Dead Child*, both of which have been much anthologized. Ironically it was his own declining health that obliged him to give up medicine and

142. Robert Bridges; oil by Charles Furse

leave Bloomsbury. Bridges remained little known until his controversial appointment as Poet Laureate in 1913. He used this new eminence to promote the work of the even less known Hopkins.

NOBEL I

The fashionable portraitist John Singer Sargent and the poet Louis MacNeice both thought he was a poseur, Auden and Eliot both admired his work, Orwell thought he was a Fascist and G.K. Chesterton called him The Man Who Knew the Fairies; it was difficult to be indifferent to W.B. Yeats (1865-1939). When he lived (1895-1919) on the second floor at 5 Woburn Walk (then 18 Woburn Buildings) the ground floor was a cobbler's shop and he was known as 'the toff', partly on account of his flamboyant dress (velvet cloak, floppy bow tie) and partly in deference to the fact that he received letters. On Monday evenings he held 'At Homes' at which he provided the Chianti and Ezra Pound dispensed it. John Masefield (1878-1967), who later lived at 18 Mecklenburgh Square, called Yeats' cramped quarters 'the most interesting room in London' and particularly remembered pride of place being given to a copy of the *Kelmscott Chaucer* printed by William Morris. Yeats was in love with the Irish nationalist Maud Gonne and treated her as his muse, though he was ultimately disenchanted by her fanaticism. Gonne rejected his sexual advances (but not those of

143. W.B. Yeats; charcoal drawing by J.S. Sargent

144. Gertrude Stein

others), but played the name part, and thus the symbol of Ireland, brilliantly, when his play *Cathleen ni Houlihan* was produced in Dublin in 1902, thereby giving birth to the Irish National Theatre Company.

Yeats actually shared his Bloomsbury garret with the novelist Olivia Shakespear - whose daughter married Ezra Pound. In 1916 he proposed to Maud Gonne after her husband had been executed in the aftermath of the Easter Rising. She refused him again but her 15-year-old daughter proposed to him; by the time he, 52, was ready to take her up on the offer she had changed her mind. In 1917 Yeats married Georgie Hyde-Lees, who combined the rare qualities of being able to organise his life and share his passion for psychical research. Their relationship decisively altered his entire approach to literary work. When Yeats finally moved out of the Woburn Walk apartment Maud Gonne moved in. Yeats went on to serve as a senator in the Irish Dail from 1922 to 1928. He was awarded the Nobel Prize for Literature in 1923.

MINOR KEYS

Yeats' towering achievements somewhat overshadow those of his other Bloomsbury contemporaries.

Charlotte Mew (1869-1928) was easily overshadowed as she was only 4 foot 10 inches tall, but Hardy considered her the best woman poet of her generation and procured her a civil list pension. Born at 10 Doughty Street, she passed a life of quiet intensity at

No. 9 Gordon Street until the death of her sister prompted her suicide.

Gertrude Stein (1874-1946) lodged briefly at 20 Bloomsbury Square in 1902, reading Trollope in the British Museum and making friends with Bertrand Russell. Neither attraction was sufficient to detain her from moving on to Paris the following year. Her self-consciously experimental writing was extremely influential in the 1920s but dismissed by the equally 'progressive' Wyndham Lewis as 'cold, black suet-pudding.... mournful and monstrous.... all fat, without nerve.' She referred to herself as 'the creative literary mind of the century'. Hemingway, whose prose was notable for its terse directness, paid her the teasing compliment of saying 'Gertrude Stein and me are just like brothers....'

W.H. Davies (1871-1940), who lost a leg jumping a train in Canada, capitalised on his loss to write *The Autobiography of a Super-Tramp* (1908) to which Shaw contributed a Preface; a prolific poet, Davies lived at 14 Great Russell Street from 1917 to 1921. By the time he moved in, Harold Monro's Poetry Bookshop at No.38 had been open for four years. Generous with both his mind and his money, Monro also edited *Poetry Review*, published Charlotte Mew and introduced Robert Frost to Edward Marsh and Ezra Pound. T.S. Eliot contributed an introduction to his collected poems, published the year after his death.

NOBEL II

In 1914 T.S. Eliot (1888-1965) settled at 28 Bedford Place at the suggestion of Ezra Pound, who secured the publication of *The Love Song of J.Alfred Prufrock* in June 1915, the month of Eliot's disastrous marriage to Vivien Haigh-Wood. Eliot never lived in Bloomsbury after that but worked in a second floor rear room at 24 Russell Square from 1925 until his death, as a director of Faber & Faber who specialised in publishing poetry. Eliot's circumspect approach to criticism caused Pound to nickname him 'Old Possum'.

A confirmed Anglican and a British citizen from 1927, Eliot endured increasingly bizarre behaviour at his wife's hands until her commitment to an asylum in 1932; on one occasion she poured a tureen of hot chocolate through the letter-box of his office door. He frequently escaped her visitations by fleeing down the fire-escape.

Dylan Thomas (1914-53), who lived for a while in Rugby Street, referred to the poet as 'Pope Eliot' and complained that his poems were 'difficult to follow unless we have an intimate knowledge of Dante, the *Golden Bough* and the weather-reports in Sanskrit'; but he was still happy to sponge off Eliot's generosity. It was left to Stephen Spender to articulate the important point behind this fatuous whine; Eliot, he observed, 'wrote a new, a really new poetry, which set up connections with the old, the really old.'

If the bumptious, scruffy, self-indulgent Dylan Thomas ridiculed Eliot's austerity and erudition, Eliot had at least the consolation of being admired by F.R. Leavis, W.H. Auden, Aldous Huxley and Virginia Woolf and being awarded both the Order of Merit and the Nobel Prize in the same year. When he died Anthony Burgess could argue that Eliot had rescued the Metaphysicals from obscurity to become A-level set texts and that:

"Spike Milligan, on a comic TV show could say 'Not with a banger but a wimpy' and most of the audience caught the reference. Weather forecasters would joke about August being 'the cruellest month.'"

Richard Aldington summed up Eliot's achievement in his biography of Ezra Pound: '... in the enormous confusion of war and post-war England, handicapped in every way... by merit, tact... and pertinacity he succeeded in doing what no other American has done - imposing his personality, taste, and even many of his opinions on literary England.'

145. T.S. Eliot; photograph by Kay Bell Reynal, 1955

146. Sir Richard Steele; engraving by Houbraken after Kneller.

147. Topham Beauclerk; engraving by Samuel Bellin after a picture by G.P. Harding.

Living off Letters

Few writers confine themselves neatly to the category of novelist, poet or dramatist and even those who do are usually critics as well. Many of the writers in this section attempted work in those fields and some even distinguished themselves by their efforts, but most are more highly valued for their contributions to other genres, such as history or the essay, or because their diaries, letters or memoirs give vivid or amusing accounts of the people they knew - or claimed to.

AUGUST AUGUSTANS

Essayist, dramatist, soldier, courtier and founding father of English journalism, Sir Richard Steele (1672-1729) lived in Bloomsbury Square for three years when it was at the height of its fashion, founding *The Spectator* and gaining and losing a seat in the Commons during that short time. Sexually profligate in his youth and financially profligate in his maturity, he was eventually driven from London by his improvidence. Macaulay summarised him as 'a scholar among rakes and a rake among scholars'.

The second Lord Chesterfield also acquired a home in Bloomsbury Square but it is the fourth (1694-1773) holder of that title who is remembered, less nowadays for his urbane letters to his son on the niceties of gentlemanly conduct, than for his failure to respond to Johnson's appeal for patronage while he laboured at compiling his famed *Dictionary*. When the *Dictionary* finally appeared Chesterfield, a kindly man whose snub was almost certainly unintentional, reviewed it warmly, provoking a response from Johnson of such measured venom that it has become a perennial candidate for any anthology of insults. When Chesterfield's letters were published after his death Johnson denounced them as teaching 'the morals of a whore and the manners of a dancing-master.' Voltaire, however, hailed Chesterfield as 'the only Englishman who ever argued for the art of pleasing as the first duty of life.' His dying words were to call for a chair for a visitor to his bed-side.

Johnson dismissed Chesterfield as having the reputation of being a Lord among wits but in truth being only a wit among Lords. He had a much higher regard for Topham Beauclerk (1739-80) a founding member of his Literary Club. The library of Beauclerk's home at 100-101 Great Russell Street was

148. *Anna Laetitia Barbauld.*

149. *William Hazlitt.*

150. *Isaac D'Israeli.*

so large that according to Horace Walpole it 'reaches halfway to Highgate... It has put the Museum's nose quite out of joint!'.

During the 1780s the western-most turning north off Great Russell Street, now Adeline Place but then Caroline Street, was home to Mrs. Anna Laetitia Barbauld (1743-1824) who was celebrated in her day for the children's books she wrote to support the work of her teacher-husband. After his suicide she composed a lengthy poem foretelling the decline of Britain, counterpoised by the rise of a prosperous and cultured America whose tourists would come to visit 'the grey ruin and the mouldering stone' of their ancestral homeland.

CRITICS AND GOSSIPS

William Hazlitt (1778-1830), the first English writer to make his living from literary and dramatic criticism, lived at his brother's house, 109 Great Russell Street from 1804 to 1807, on the eve of his rise to fame. His *View of the English Stage* (1818) contains perceptive appreciations of Kean, Kemble, Siddons and other Bloomsbury theatricals and his *Spirit of the Age* (1825) offers shrewd pen-portraits of Bentham, Godwin and Lamb, among many others. T.S. Eliot thought he 'had perhaps the most uninteresting mind of all our distinguished critics.'

Eliot would probably have thought Isaac D'Israeli (1766-1848) unworthy even of such contemptuous

151. *A former home of Isaac D'Israeli, in Theobalds Road, Holborn. It was here that the future prime minister, Benjamin Disraeli, was born.*

152. *Thomas Babington Macaulay; painting by Sir Francis Grant.*

dismissal. A dilettante known mainly for his rag-bag *Curiosities of Literature* (6 vols 1791-1834) , he lived at 6 Bloomsbury Square from 1817 to 1829 in order to be near the British Museum. Byron enjoyed reading him, however, and encouraged the one consistent thread in his meanderings, research into the qualities that make a creative writer. It is ironic therefore that the runaway success of *Vivian Grey*, the first novel written by his son, future Prime Minister Benjamin Disraeli, came as a complete shock to him.

Thomas Babington Macaulay (1800-59) whose magisterial *History of England* (1849-55) was an instant best-seller and has never been out of print since, won overnight celebrity with an *Edinburgh Review* essay on Milton published when he was only 25 and living at 50 Great Ormond Street. Henry Crabb Robinson (1775-1867), who lived at 30 Russell Square from 1839 to 1867, was yet another Bloomsbury lawyer with literary leanings. A founder of University College and friend of Hazlitt, he was a tireless in his attendance at lectures and soirees, making his diaries an invaluable source for the literary historian.

The combative Eliza Lynn Linton (1822-98) represents quite the opposite literary type from the clubbable Robinson. *Azeth the Eygptian* (1846), the first of her 35 novels, was the product of dutiful study in the British Museum. By the time she came to live at 28 Gower Street, she had made her mark as the first woman feature writer on a national newspaper, the prestigious *Morning Chronicle*. Her anti-feminist features, appearing in the *Saturday Review* from 1866 onwards, made her notorious. In *The Girl of the Period* she lambasted young women for wearing short skirts and too much make-up and only being interested in men, money and themselves. Conspicuously kind in personal life, she gave such freedom to her vitriolic pen as to collect an impressively large and comprehensive set of enemies. Her posthumous memoir, *My Literary Life*, contains a remarkably scathing assault on George Eliot.

JACKS OF ALL TRADES

Bloomsbury's abundance of publishers, bookshops, lecture halls and literary 'characters', not to mention its proximity to 'legal London' and 'Theatreland' make it a convenient location for the grubbing wordsmith on the look-out for contacts and 'colour'. The flamboyant journalist, George A. Sala (1828-96), was a regular contributor to *Household Words* while Dickens was living in Tavistock Square. Travel-writer, novelist and columnist for the *Daily Telegraph*, he spent his last years at 46 Mecklenburgh Square.

E.V. Lucas (1868-1938) who contributed to *Punch*, edited Lamb's writings and churned out anthologies, romances and travel books, lived at 5 Great James Street in the 1890s. His memoirs of the book

153. *George Augustus Sala; caricature by 'Ape' in* Vanity Fair, *September 1875.*

world are entitled *Reading, Writing and Remembering* (1932), which proved to be a formula for survival, if not success. No.4 Great James Street was home to Frank Swinnerton (1884-1982) who worked his way up from officeboy to editor at Chatto & Windus and himself wrote novels set in contemporary London. Literary critic of *The Observer* and President of the Royal Literary Fund, he was a good friend of Arnold Bennett and, more or less as a consequence of that, a dismissive critic of Virginia Woolf.

A.J.A. Symons (1900-41), bibliophile, dandy and epicure, lived at 17 Bedford Square. He escaped a humble background to establish the First Edition Club and the Wine and Food Society. He also wrote a biography of that equally odd fish Frederick Rolfe, self-styled Baron Corvo. His best work was his own epitaph 'A.J.A.S. - ALAS'.

154. *R.H. Tawney*

James Agate (1877-1947), sometime inhabitant of 14 Doughty Street, wrote drama criticism for *The Sunday Times*, film criticism for the *Tatler* and book reviews for the *Daily Express*. His nine-volume auto-biographical saga records literary and theatrical personalities of his day and is appropriately entitled *Ego*.

The socialist historian R.H. Tawney (1880-1962), sometime inhabitant of 21 Mecklenburgh Square seems rather a pious plodder set beside this raffish crew. A lineal intellectual descendant of Ruskin, Morris and the Christian Socialists, Tawney was a member of the executive committee of the Workers' Educational Association for 42 years. He became Professor of Economic History at the London School of Economics in 1931, five years after the publication of his most seminal work *Religion and the Capitalism*.

Helen Hanff, author of the highly successful *84 Charing Cross Road*, a chatty account of her twenty year transatlantic correspondence with a bookseller at that address, stayed at the Kenilworth Hotel when its British edition was published. She was so besotted by her Bloomsbury surroundings that she never got to see the Tower of London. The publicity department of her publisher, Andre Deutsch, arranged so many interviews and invitations that the hotel staff dubbed her 'The Duchess of Bloomsbury Street' - which became the title of her next book.

PUBLISHERS

Law, learning and leisure have been the chief preoccupations of Bloomsbury's inhabitants, but as books have always been central to these pursuits, it is perhaps not surprising that Bloomsbury is quintessentially the home of publishers and book-sellers.

The name of Luke Hansard (1752-1858) has become synonymous with the verbatim record of parliamentary debates. Printer to the House of Commons from 1798, he lived at 4 Gower Street from 1808-1810. Thomas Cadell (d.1802), Hansard's near-contemporary, lived in Bloomsbury Place. His main claim to fame was to have published the first edition of Gibbon's *Decline and Fall of the Roman Empire*. Charles Knight (1791-1873), who lived at 26 Bloomsbury Square, became publisher to the Society for the Diffusion of Useful Knowledge and specialised in the large-scale production of cheap editions of popular 'classics' and illustrated histories.

Bedford Square has perhaps the best claim to be considered the focal centre of publishing, having housed, or currently housing, the offices of Frederick Warne (publishers of Beatrix Potter), Jonathan Cape, Michael Joseph, Hodder & Stoughton, Heinemann Educational, British Museum Publications and the Publishers' Association. Thames and Hudson and the Good Book Guide are located just around the corner.

155. Charles Knight

Bloomsbury - as a community, rather than an area - has also given birth to two small but highly significant publishing-houses of its own, both committed to producing books of high technical merit, often of avant-garde content, untrammelled by merely commercial considerations.

The Hogarth Press, established by Leonard and Virginia Woolf in 1917 at their Richmond home, Hogarth House, moved to Bloomsbury in 1924. The Hogarth Press was blitzed out in the war and Virginia's suicide followed shortly afterwards. Apart from Virginia Woolf's own work, it was the first to publish the short stories of Katherine Mansfield (the only writer whose style Virginia confessed to envy) and T.S. Eliot's *The Waste Land*. In 1926 the Hogarth Press brought out the first novel of poet-publisher William Plomer (1903-73), a long-term Bloomsbury inhabitant whose poems include *The Planes of Bedford Square* and *A Ticket for the Reading Room*.

The Nonesuch Press was established in 1923 by typographer Francis Meynell (1891-1975) and novelist David Garnett (1892-1981). In 1936 it published *The Nonesuch Century*, a celebration of its first hundred titles, with the assistance of A.J.A. Symons, who was no doubt attracted by the self-congratulatory tone of the project.

BOOKSELLERS

Publishing books is one kind of business, selling them quite another. Bloomsbury now has bookshops specialising in subjects as varied as building, Buddhism and the Bloomsbury group, medicine, mysticism and the Maghreb. Scholars around the world start with fond recognition at the name of Luzac's, Probsthain's, Collett's or Lewis's.

Charles Edward Mudie (d.1890) blazed the way, setting up his shop in Southampton Row in 1840. Soon he was building up a profitable new sideline lending out textbooks to the young gentlemen of University College - until it dawned on him that the real money lay in lending novels to the general public. By 1852 he was ready to move to new premises at the corner of Museum Street and New Oxford Strret. He now claimed to have 120,000 volumes in circulation with a million more in reserve, serving 20,000 subscribers and making 1,000 exchanges every day. 'Mudie's Select Library' was good news for publishers. When Macaulay's *History of England* came out he took 2,500 copies, while Livingston's *Travels in Africa* merited 3,250.

Trail-blazing Mudie was at least the son of a bookseller. Una Dillon had no previous experience when she borrowed £800 to buy a failing business in Store Street in 1937. Whatever magic it takes to build up a bookshop through a depression, a war and years of rationing, Una Dillon (1903-93) had it. Dillon's became the official University of London bookshop

156. *Mudie's Library in New Oxford Street.*

157. *Una Dillon.*

and in 1956 moved to its present site. Since then the 1907 Gothic fantasy designed as a shopping-parade by Fitzroy Doll, architect of the Hotel Russell, has been transformed into one of the capital's finest bookshops and the Dillons name has become the emblem of a national chain.

158. *The H.K. Lewis bookshop at 140 Gower Street in the 1940s.*

The Theatricals

THICK-SKINNED AND THIN-SKINNED

Shrill-voiced, self-satisfied Colly Cibber (1671-1757), nicknamed 'Hatchet Face' in his youth, was born in what is now Southampton Place and lived there again from 1714 to 1720. Most of his thirty-plus plays were flops - Cibber coldly likened them to his children, who were multitudinous, and often short-lived; nevertheless he was made Poet Laureate in 1730, an appointment which prompted the observation:

'In merry old England it once was a rule
The King had his Poet, and also his Fool.
But now we're so frugal, I'd have you to know it,
That Cibber can serve both for Fool and for Poet.'

Cibber attributed this barb to the venomous Alexander Pope (1688-1744), who also advised him:-

'Cibber! write all thy Verses upon Glasses,
The only way to save 'em from our A.......s.'

One of Pope's best-known works, the *Dunciad*, a lengthy verse-satire on Dullness, was originally composed to revenge the author on his exact contemporary, Lewis Theobald (1688-1744), the founding father of Shakespeare studies, whose meticulous study of original sources had exposed Pope's sloppiness as

159. Colley Cibber, after the painting by Venloo.

an editor of the Bard. (Theobald, coincidentally, was a near-neighbour of Cibber's, residing in Wyan's Court, a turning off Great Russell Street, now long vanished.) Revising the *Dunciad* fifteen years after its first anonymous publication, Pope replaced Theobald with Cibber as its 'hero'. Their feud continued literally to the death, Pope signing it off in epigram:-

'Quoth Cibber to Pope, tho' in Verse you foreclose,
I'll have the last word, for by God I'll write Prose.
Poor Colley, thy Reas'ning is none of the strongest,
For know, the last Word is the word that lasts longest.'

Johnson conceded Cibber's talent for comedy but held him in contempt as a man - 'It is wonderful that a man, who for forty years had lived with the great and the witty, should have acquired so ill the talents of conversation; and he had but half to furnish: for one half of what he said was oaths.' Cibber's most enduring theatrical achievement was an adaptation of *Richard III* which was long preferred to the original. Dramatist Richard Cumberland (1732-1811) has been characterised as 'the most typical exponent of the eighteenth-century style which received its death-blow at the hands of Sheridan.' His speciality was sentimental domestic comedies, though his best-known works were *The West Indian*, which Garrick produced to great acclaim and *The Jew*, one of the first plays to plead the cause of Jewry; it provided fine parts for the leading actors of the day and was translated into several languages. Ultra-sensitive to criticism, Cumberland suffered the torture of caricature by becoming Sir Fretful Plagiary in Sheridan's *The Critic*. He died at 30 Bedford Place, then but newly-built.

TRAGEDIANS, BUFFOONS AND SCANDAL

John Philip Kemble (1757-1823), the greatest male tragedian of his generation, lived at 12 Adeline Place in the 1790s and at 89 Great Russell Street from 1808 to 1823. Conceding his impressive stage presence, critics yet thought him too studied. Hazlitt condemned him as 'a petrification of sentiment.... an icicle upon the bust of Tragedy', while Leigh Hunt observed that 'he never pulls out his handkerchief without a design upon the audience' and concluded that 'He was no more to be compared to his sister than stone is to flesh and blood.'

Kemble's sister was Sarah Siddons (1755-1831) who, at the height of her fame, lived at 14 Gower St. from 1784 to 1789. They shared seven other theatrical siblings but none approached her standing. Fanny Burney, who had been enchanted by Garrick, was enthralled by Mrs.Siddons - 'sublime, elevated and solemn', while Hazlitt dubbed her 'the stateliest ornament of the public mind.'

160. *Sarah Siddons; oil sketch by George Romney.*

161. *John Philip Kemble; by Sir Thomas Lawrence.*

What the redoubtable Kembles were to tragedy Jack Bannister (1760-1836) was to comic drollery. Lamb thought him consummate in his playing of an audience. He died at 65 Gower Street. His contemporary, Charles Mathews (1776-1835), gifted with an amazing memory and effortless powers of mimicry, mastered four hundred parts and pioneered the one-man show, performing a bewildering variety of comic roles in quick-fire succession. The youthful Dickens was an avid fan: 'I went to some theatre every night... and always to see Mathews whenever he played', and claimed to have committed three or four of Mathew's *At Homes* to memory. Mathews eventually settled at 101 Great Russell Street, where he wrote his autobiography.

Buried in St George's Gardens lies the leading comedienne of their day, Julia Betterton Glover (1779-1850). Despite long experience in 'breeches parts' and the natural advantage of a huge waistline, she was crucified by the critics when she attempted Falstaff. Publicity of a different sort attended 'actress' Mary Anne Clarke (1776-1852) of 31 Tavistock Place. Her involvement with the 'Grand Old' Duke of York blew into a scandal which led to his dismissal from the army on charges of corruption. She was imprisoned for libels contained in her first volume of memoirs and paid £10,000 and a pension for not publishing a second one. The romantic novelist Daphne du Maurier was her direct descendant.

162. *Mary Anne Clarke*

POLISHED PROFESSIONALS

Charles Kean (1811-68), who lived at 3, Torrington Square, was the son of the great Edmund, with less of his father's dramatic genius but a greater gift for the practical business of theatrical production. While managing the Princess's Theatre in nearby Oxford St. he pioneered the use of lime-light and sponsored the debut of Ellen Terry at the age of nine.

Impresario Richard D'Oyly Carte (1844-1901), builder of the Savoy Theatre and the adjoining Savoy Hotel, lived at 71 Russell Square before moving across to the Adelphi Terrace in 1888.

(Walter) Weedon Grossmith (1852-1919) is now chiefly remembered as the co-author and illustrator of *Diary of a Nobody*, a telling satire on the daily round of Holloway bank clerk Henry Pooter, whose obsession with respectability amounted to virtual paranoia; but Grossmith was also a successful dramatist. He lived at 1 Bedford Square from 1902 until his death, while his brother and collaborator George (1847-1912) lived at 58 Russell Square. George made his name with Gilbert and Sullivan but later left the Savoy opera company to become a solo entertainer, accompanying himself at the piano and chronicling his experiences in an autobiography knowingly entitled *A Society Clown*.

164. Charles Kean

163. Weedon Grossmith

165. George Grossmith

Scottish drama critic, William Archer (1856-1924), lived at 34 Great Ormond Street in the 1890s. A severe intellectual with an astringent sense of humour, he became a firm friend of the like-minded Bernard Shaw (who then lived in Fitzroy Square). Archer's major achievement was to translate and promote the plays of Ibsen, eventually publishing a complete edition of his works in eleven volumes. In 1913 Archer became the first President of the newly-founded Critics' Circle.

Sir Johnston Forbes-Robertson (1853-1937) enjoyed almost forty years of uninterrupted stage success. A protege of Irving, he eventually succeeded him both as manager of the Lyceum and unchallenged Hamlet of his day. He was also hailed for his performance as The Stranger in The *Passing of the Third Floor Back* (1908), the best stage work from the pen of Jerome K. Jerome. Shaw, no easy man to please, saw a true nobility in his classic roles. Sir Johnston Forbes-Robertson lived at 22 Bedford Square. His contempo-

166. Sir Johnston Forbes-Robertson

167. Seymour Hicks

rary and neighbour at No. 53, Sir Seymour Hicks (1871-1949) made his stage debut in Islington at the age of sixteen and went on to produce London's first revue, to pioneer entertainment for the troops in the Great War and to prove himself equally adept in straight plays and the music hall. While living in Bedford Square he opened the Hicks Theatre in Shaftesbury Avenue: it is now the Globe. He frequently co-starred with his wife, Ellaline Terriss (1871-1971).

RADA

Forbes-Robertson was a leading member of the founding committee of the Royal Academy of Dramatic Art, which moved to Gower Street in 1904. Its Royal Charter was granted in 1920 and in 1921 the Prince of Wales became its patron after opening its new theatre in Malet Street. Energetic fund-raising efforts by Bernard Shaw enabled the premises to be reconstructed in 1931 but they were virtually destroyed by bombing in 1941. The present Vanbrugh Theatre was opened by the Queen Mother, Chancellor of the University of London, in 1954. Shaw bequeathed a third of his royalties for the benefit of RADA.

The site now occupied by the School of Hygiene and Tropical Medicine in Keppel Street was originally acquired by trustees for the establishment of a National Theatre but this plan was abandoned in 1923 for lack of funds.

168. *The 'Shakespeare Hut' in Keppel Street. The site was originally purchased by the Shakespeare Committee on which to build the National Theatre, but with the outbreak of the First World War the Committee let it to the YWCA rent-free for the erection of a building for the entertainment of soldiers. The London School of Hygiene and Tropical Medicine now covers the site.*

169. *Trevithick's 'Catch-me-if-you-can' demonstration railway, at the northern end of Gower Street in 1802.*

170. Henry Cavendish

Science and Technology

Bloomsbury contributions to science have been few but distinguished.

Mining engineer Richard Trevithick (1771-1833) pioneered the development of high-pressure steam-engines ten years before George Stephenson and gave the earliest public demonstration of the railway locomotive on a patch of waste ground at the north end of Gower Street in 1802. A fruitless foray to South America, where he hoped to use steam-power to create a new Eldorado by opening up silver mines cost him a wasted decade and his entire fortune. By the time he returned home penniless in 1827 the palm had passed to his rival Stephenson.

No greater contrast of temperament could be imagined than between the self-made, macho mining engineers Trevithick and Stephenson and the reclusive, aristocratic Henry Cavendish (1731-1810), who lived at 11 Bedford Square from 1786 until his death. Lord Brougham observed of Cavendish that 'his whole existence was in his laboratory or in his library' and Sir Joseph Banks, President of the Royal Society, opined that 'he probably uttered fewer words in the course of his life than any man who has lived to four score years.' Attendance at Banks's monthly scientific gatherings in nearby Soho Square was one of the few social occasions which Cavendish steeled himself to endure. Normally he was so shy that he ordered his dinner from his servants by leaving a note for them. And dinner was invariably frugal. When a servant ventured to suggest that a single leg of lamb might be insufficient for a group of guests his response was to order two legs of lamb. Yet when he died he left over a million pounds to his relatives.

Ironically the name of the reclusive Cavendish has become known around the world since Cambridge University decided to name its main science laboratories after him. And the honour is well-merited. Cavendish was the first to discover that water consisted of hydrogen and oxygen, the first to describe the composition of nitric acid and the first to isolate the inert gas, argon, though he was unaware that he had done so. He was also interested in electrical phenomena and devised the principles of an experiment to determine the density of the earth. (The experiment was actually carried out by another Bloomsbury resident, Francis Baily, President of the

171. Francis Baily

172. *'House in Tavistock Place in which Mr Baily weighed the Earth'.*

173. *'Room in which Mr Baily weighed the Earth'.*

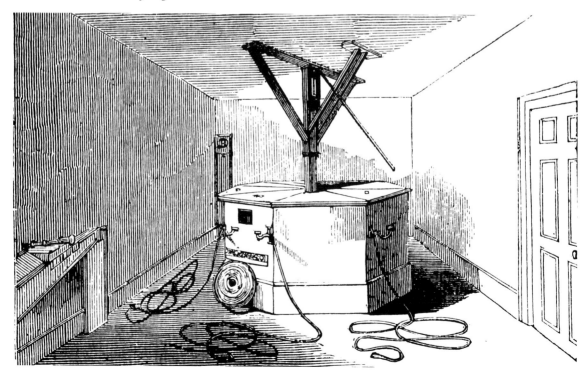

Royal Astronomical Society, at 37 Tavistock Place, where he lived from 1825 to 1844).

Charles Darwin (1809-82) returned from his five year round the world voyage as naturalist on the *Beagle* in 1836, became Secretary of the Geological Society in 1838 and, marrying his cousin, Emma Wedgwood, that same year, moved into his first marital home at what was then 12 Upper Gower Street on New Year's day 1839. The rent was 'extraordinarily low' and the furnishings extraordinarily hideous. Darwin's son later described it as 'a small, commonplace London house with a drawing-room in front and a small room behind, in which they lived for the sake of quietness.' This was an important consideration for Darwin, who valued the sanctuary of his ninety foot rear garden. Writing to a friend in October 1839 he emphasised: 'We are living a life of extreme quietness... and if one is quiet in London there is nothing like its quietness - there is a grandeur about its smoky fogs, and the dull distant sounds of cabs and coaches; in fact you may perceive I am becoming a thorough-paced Cockney.'

In fact Darwin was plagued by recurrent illness and migraines, which affected the progress of his researches. He was already working hard on organising the evidence which would substantiate the theory of evolution he would publish twenty years later as *The Origin of Species* . The birth of his first child set off another train of observation and enquiry which issued in a book on *Expression of the Emotions*.

In 1842, at the height of the Chartist agitations, Darwin was alarmed by the sight of troops marching up Gower Street on their way to Euston station and the troubled industrial North. The family moved out that year and settled at Down in Kent, where he remained for the rest of his life. When he died he was hailed as 'the Newton of the realm of living things' and 'the incorporated ideal of the man of science'. The site of his Gower Street home is now occupied, very appropriately, by the biological laboratories of University College.

174. *Charles Darwin; oil painting by John Collier*

The Traders

Business has never really been the business of Bloomsbury.

Bloomsbury Market folded by 1780 and the site was so radically redeveloped that only the name of Barter Street really recalls its existence. From 1836 to 1900 there *was* a Bloomsbury Savings Bank at 30 Montague Street, but the very idea of such blatant commercialism was so distasteful that the building could scarcely be distinguished from the houses next to it and, even so, was required to provide a waiting-room lest customers should mill around untidily outside.

The construction of New Oxford Street in the 1840s established a commercial corridor of prestigious and specialist establishments along Bloomsbury's southern fringe - Harris and Sons, dealers in antique furniture; Camerer, Cuss and Company, jewellers and clockmakers; Imhof's, dealers in musical instruments, who sold the first gramophone in 1896; and James Smith and Sons, suppliers of umbrellas to Gladstone and Lord Curzon.

Towering above them all, in turnover terms at least, was pharmacist Thomas Holloway (1800-83), who had but modest success until he hit on the notion of using newspaper advertising on an unprecedented scale to promote his pills and potions. Between 1842 and 1877 he raised his annual publicity budget from £5,000 to £40,000. The fortune he made was largely disbursed on charitable causes - most notably the foundation of Royal Holloway College, for the education of young ladies, at Egham, Surrey. Designed in the flamboyant style of a Loire valley chateau, it was opened by Queen Victoria herself in 1886 and became part of the University of London in 1900. It was merged with Bedford College in the 1980s.

Great Russell Street gradually became commercialised through catering to the whims of visitors to the British Museum, and Southampton Row followed this trend with the building of its major hotels and the increased traffic flow resulting from the construction of Kingsway in the decade before the Great War.

The as yet unwritten story of Marchmont Street is, however, more truly representative of the nature of Bloomsbury traders as a whole. It began as a largely residential thoroughfare. *Boyle's Court Guide* for 1820 lists no less than fourteen persons of quality among its residents, including a surgeon and a solicitor. By 1829 the number had already fallen to nine, five years later to seven and by 1840 to a mere four, whose marginal claims to gentility were represented by a dentist and, more dubiously, an artist. The same year's edition of *Robson's Commercial Directory of London* shows that not only were many premises by

175. New Oxford Street c1878; watercolour attributed to J. Absolon.

176. *The original James Smith umbrella shop in New Oxford Street, in a terrace of buildings later the site of Glave's department store (see Illustration 181).*

177. *'Mr Gattie who lived for many years at the fishmonger's at the corner of Marchmont and Burton Streets, who acted at Tottenham Street theatre'. (See also Illustration 18)*

then occupied at ground floor level for retail purposes but also that most of the rest were being used as workshops of one sort or another. The rag trade was the most prominent local business, employing six milliners, two staymakers, two tailors and a dressmaker, a haberdasher and a dyer, with other aspects of personal adornment providing a livelihood for three hairdressers, two jewellers, a goldsmith, a furrier and a bootmaker. Gastronomic needs were catered for by four butchers, four cheesemongers, four grocers, three dairymen-cowkeepers, a poulterer, a fishmonger, a baker, a dealer in potatoes and an 'Italian warehouseman'. Other retail establishments included three chemists, two tobacconists, two linen-drapers, two booksellers and an ironmonger. Wholesaling was represented by dealers in toys and china. The furniture trades provided employment for two upholsterers and a carver and gilder. Other craftsmen included four plumbers, a brushmaker and a cooper. In other words, in a short street of some sixty units, more than thirty different businesses were being carried on.

178. *James Smith founded his famous umbrella, cane and walking-stick store in 1830. The present premises at 53 New Oxford Street are a magnificent survival of a high-Victorian shop. Despite the vagaries of fashion and invention, the basic Smith umbrella still sells in large quantities as do canes and whips, though canes had their heyday in World War I when regimental 'swagger' canes were an essential item for fashionable soldiers. This picture is undated but was probably taken at the turn of this century.*

179. *A wet winter evening in the 1920s, and a bookshop in Sicilian Avenue.*

HENRY GLAVE'S

Park and River Frocks,
Travelling and
Boating Costumes,
Tasteful Millinery,
Original Coats and
Jackets,
Lingerie and Corsets,
Sunshades and
Umbrellas,
Silks, Satins & Velvets
Home and
Foreign Dresses,
Household Linens,
Cretonnes and
Curtains,
Hosiery, Gloves, Lace,
Flowers. and
Trimmings,
Haberdashery and
Fancy Goods.

All Goods marked in plain figures and sold for Cash.

PATTERNS AND FASHION PLATES SENT POST FREE.

HENRY GLAVE,

80, 82, 84, 86, 88, 94, 96, NEW OXFORD STREET, W.C.

180. *By the end of the 1st World War Henry Glave, linen draper, had accumulated in the time-honoured tradition a number of shops along New Oxford Street, not all of them linked, as his business expanded. Between the wars the block was demolished and a purpose-built store was erected, but by then such trade had moved decisively west along Oxford Street and Glave's store became a commercial white elephant..*

The Marchmont Street entry in the *Post Office Directory* for 1877 reveals a similar range of occupations catering for local needs, plus more specialised businesses such as a watchmaker, a sign-writer and manufacturers of umbrellas and blacking. There is also a Post Office with savings bank and telegraph facilities. The cosmopolitan character of the commercial community is attested by the presence of confectioner Pietro Corsini and linen-draper Solomon Rosenbloom. Fifty years on both those businesses were still trading under the same names. Specialist 'ladies tailors' and hairdressers were also there in the 1920s, just as they had been a century before. But the existence of two dealers in antique furniture implies a move up-market, while the two laundries may well have served the legions of local boarding-houses. The presence of local branches of retail chains such as Pearks', Home and Colonial, Express Dairy and Unwin's wine merchants foreshadows the penetration of impersonal multiples into an area traditionally dominated by the small family-run business.

For one conspicuously large family business relocation to Bloomsbury was to prove a total disaster. Glave's had traded successfully as a linen-draper in the area for half a century when it moved to brand-new, purpose-built premises at the western end of New Oxford Street at the end of the 1920s. For whatever reasons the move proved fatal to the business.

181. *The Glave department store, a building which still exists in New Oxford Street,*

A Place to Stay

The poets Cowper and Gray took lodgings in Southampton Row in the 1750s. A century later Edward
Fitzgerald habitually stayed in rooms in Bloomsbury
Street. He also had the additional option of accommodation at Euston which, in 1839, had offered its
travellers the convenience of staying at the first of
London's railway hotels. The same decade saw the
opening of London's first temperance hotels -
Bloomsbury soon became noted for them. Perhaps
that - and the presence of the British Museum - was
what attracted temperance promoter and group-
travel pioneer Thomas Cook to establish his first
London office at 59 Great Russell Street in 1862.
Forbidden by the terms of his lease to have any trade
sign beyond a name on the door, he made the best he
could of it by entitling his establishment Cook's
British Museum Boarding House. In 1866 he ex-
tended his services to clients by offering them a hotel
reservation facility.

Contemporaries appear to have felt that the chang-
ing balance between residential and commercial property in the Bloomsbury area threatened to degrade its
character. The *Builder* commented as early as 1844:
'... houses are now being rapidly deserted - are
converted or converting into shops, lodging-houses
and chambers, and in a few years, when age begins
to stamp its mark upon them, the last traces of
aristocratic, commercial or professional opulence
will vanish from among them.'

Even exclusive Bedford Square was not immune
from the trend. No.14, once the home of a Lord
Mayor, had become a lodging-house by the 1840s.

The Building News of 1861 noted that the imposing
houses facing onto the squares had large rooms
which made convenient offices for lawyers, doctors
and other professional men; it predicted an inevitable conversion of such family dwellings to occupational use.

By the 1870s John Bourne, steward of the Bedford
estate, felt that what he called 'lodging-house dry rot'
had got such a grip on Gower Street that only the
most draconian policy could restore its original character as a street of gentlemen's residences. He therefore instituted a policy of offering new leases only to
private residents and demanding repairs and altera-
tions so extensive as to be far beyond the resources of
penny-pinching landladies. The result was empty
property and, after a tenacious campaign of more
than a decade, surrender to the apparently inevitable.

If Bloomsbury was no longer fashionable, however, this did not mean that it had ceased to be
respectable. A guide-book of 1888 reassured readers
that: 'Some of the quiet squares in the Bloomsbury

*182 & 183. Two hotels demonstrating the transition of
Bloomsbury houses into hotels. Above, the Gower Hotel next to
Euston Square station, and below, St Anthony at 2 & 3
Torrington Square, both early in this century.*

184. *For those who could not afford hotels the traditional pub accommodation was still available, at such places as The Friend at Hand in Herbrand Street.*

185. *The West Central Hotel in Southampton Row. It boasted a Baedeker mention and electric light, but no intoxicants.*

186. *The Imperial Hotel in Russell Square is partly built on the right of the picture. The adjacent collection of original houses of the Square is already earmarked with a proud clarity as the site for its extension. See Illustration 190 for its fully built form.*

district are very desirable resting-places in London, and we know of more than one boarding-house in this quarter at which we ourselves should consider it a privilege to stay.'

Nevertheless potential visitors were warned that their fellow-guests might be a very mixed bunch: 'There are boarding-houses in Bloomsbury where are to be found medical and other students of both sexes and several nationalities, American folk passing through London, literary persons 'up' for a week or two's reading at the British Museum, brides and bridegrooms from the provinces, Bohemians pure and simple, and the restless gentlemen who are 'something in the City', but no one knows what....'

HOTELS AND HOSTELRIES

Perhaps it was the presence of 'Bohemians' that explains the opening of the Vienna Cafe at 24-28 New Oxford Street in 1885. Owned by the Anglo-Austrian Confectionery Co., it offered clients not only a tempting array of pastries but also the opportunity to linger over chess or the newspapers.

At the same time a new kind of lavishly-appointed public house began to colonise prominent corner-sites. The Marquis Cornwallis, The Sun, The Rugby Tavern and the Norfolk Arms are good examples. The ancient Horseshoe on Tottenham Court Road

up-graded itself from way-side tavern to hotel status and even boasted the services of a genuine American bar-man to mix cocktails. The Apollo, at the corner of Tottenham Court Road and Torrington Place, was one of the most splendid. Adorned with terra cotta statues of the Nine Muses, it was opened in 1898, demolished in 1961. Euterpe, muse of music, stands forlorn in St George's Gardens to this day.

These innovations were the harbingers of a new phase of development as guest-houses converted from family homes were forced to face competition from large-scale, purpose-built hotels, such as the Thackeray (1895), bang opposite the British Museum and the Bonnington, the Bedford and the West Central on Southampton Row. The latter boasted a *Baedeker* commendation, lifts, 'electric light throughout' and a guaranteed absence of 'intoxicants'. The National Hotel in Upper Bedford Place went much further, offering such exotic facilities as an indoor swimming bath, a 'Dutch garden and fish pond' and a one hundred and fifty-foot rifle-range.

The Hotel Russell (1900), overlooked Russell Square itself. Designed in a flamboyant French Gothic by the Bedford estate's own architect, Charles Fitzroy Doll, the Russell proclaimed its aspiration to an international clientele on its very facade, which was adorned at first-floor height with a terra-cotta frieze of na-

187.   *The downstairs restaurant in the Vienna Café in New Oxford Street, c1885*

tional symbols, from the American eagle to the Japanese chrysanthemum. It was an immediate success. A *Directory* of London's American residents, published in 1901, lists the Russell as an accommodation address for half a dozen families, alongside such other fashionable hotels as the Savoy and the Cecil.

The Imperial, next to the Russell, and also designed by Doll was even more extravagantly ornate in its interpretation of the Gothic. It was intended to be built in three phases. The first was completed in 1907 and the second in 1911 but the third was never built. Even so it could offer its clients a fabulous suite of Turkish baths, famed throughout the capital. The Imperial was demolished in the 1960s and replaced with an austere modern successor. The ghost of its celebrated baths is memorialized in a handsome marble sign embedded in the pavement at the junction of Russell Square and Guilford Street.

188. The National Hotel in Upper Bedford Place offered a swimming pool, rifle-range and a Dutch Garden.

189. The Royal Hotel in Woburn Place.

190. *The Imperial Hotel in Russell Square, in its Edwardian heyday.*

191. *The Reading and Writing Room of the Hotel Russell.*

The 'Bloomsberries'

Much - in some opinions, far too much - has been written about the so-called 'Bloomsbury Group', both by themselves, by those whose lives they touched and by cohorts of academic and literary commentators seeking to trace their influence or evaluate their impact. The validity of the term 'group' is itself contested - or else it is alleged that by the time they were recognised as a 'group' they had ceased to be one.

The Bloomsbury 'network', shall we say?, originated in another network - of Cambridge cliques. In a sense its intellectual ancestry can be traced back to the 1820s when F.D. Maurice (the Christian Socialist originator of the Working Men's College) founded the 'Apostles' a semi-secret student society which met weekly for discussion. Three 'embryos' were normally elected to its elite ranks each year. Illustrious early members included Edward Fitzgerald, Tennyson and (Sir) Leslie Stephen, editor of the monumental *Dictionary of National Biography*. Later members included Roger Fry, Desmond MacCarthy, E.M. Forster, Lytton Strachey, Leonard Woolf, Saxon Sydney-Turner and John Maynard Keynes - all of whom subsequently became members of the Bloomsbury circle. In 1899 Strachey, Woolf and Sydney-Turner, together with Thoby Stephen (son of Sir Leslie) and Clive Bell founded the 'Midnight Society', a reading-circle.

Woolf, Strachey, MacCarthy, Forster and Bertrand Russell were all pupils or friends of the Cambridge philosopher G.E. Moore (1873-1958), whose *Principia Ethica* (published in 1903) had repercussions far beyond the technical realm of moral philosophy. The *Principia* did not, of course, 'cause' the 'Bloomsburys' in any crude sense (they were often consciously unconventional but never crude), but their creed, if they can be said to have had one, was succinctly described in one of Moore's central tenets: 'By far the most valuable things ...are ...the pleasures of human intercourse and the enjoyment of beautiful objects; ... it is they ....that form the rational ultimate end of social progress.'

The catalyst which created Bloomsbury as a loose community of like-minded aesthetes was the death in 1904 of Sir Leslie Stephen. His two daughters, Vanessa and Virginia, moved into 46 Gordon Square and began to entertain the Cambridge friends of their brother, Thoby, with sparkling conversation and rather dull refreshments.

Thoby died suddenly in Greece in 1906 as a result of typhoid. Vanessa, distraught, found consolation in marriage to Clive Bell. In 1907 Virginia and another brother, Adrian, moved over to Fitzroy Square. After that it all begins to get rather complicated; but

192. Virginia Woolf

193. Duncan Grant

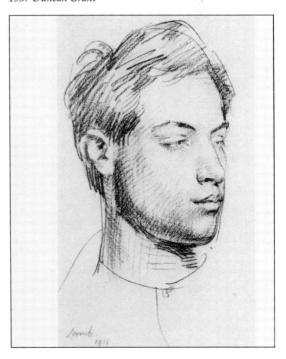

the Bloomsbury network can be broadly said to have consisted of two overlapping circles whose primary interests were respectively literary and artistic and to which a penumbra of rather less aesthetically-minded intellectuals, such as the economists Keynes and Shove, the mathematician, H.T. Norton, and the Treasury mandarin Saxon Sydney-Turner, more or less attached themselves.

THE WRITERS

The most important of the writers was Virginia Stephen, who became Virginia Woolf on her marriage to Leonard in 1912, having turned down, among others, Lytton Strachey. She never had any formal schooling. When her mother died in 1895 she had the first of several mental breakdowns; another followed the death of her father. In 1905 she began a life-long association as a reviewer for the *Times Literary Supplement*. By November 1911 she was sharing 38 Brunswick Square with her brother Adrian, the economist John Maynard Keynes and the painter Duncan Grant. A year after her marriage she attempted suicide but was saved by the prompt action of Geoffrey, the doctor brother of J.M. Keynes, who was also living at No. 38. (He was a close friend of Rupert Brooke, married a grand-daughter of Darwin and designed books for the *Nonesuch Press*.)

In 1915 Virginia's first novel, *The Way Out*, was published by one of her half-brothers, Gerald Duckworth. In the course of the next decade there

followed more novels and the foundation of the Hogarth Press. Her major works, *To the Lighthouse* and *The Waves*, appeared in 1927 and 1931 respectively. In 1934 came *Walter Sickert, A Conversation* and an invitation to write a biography of art critic Roger Fry, which she worked on for five years but never finished. Her suicide (by drowning) was motivated not by the war but the conviction that she was once again slipping into insanity. Her work was admired by Auden and Spender but not by Cyril Connolly, Edith Sitwell or F.R. Leavis. Frank Swinnerton summed it up as 'very clever, very ingenious, but creatively unimportant... there was nothing in it for those who did not pride themselves upon intellectual superiority to the herd.' In the view of her biographer, Michael Rosenthal, such middlebrow contempt was typical of those who saw her as the apotheosis of Bloomsbury values - socially snobbish, sexually effete, morally perverse, politically unaware and economically parasitic. This made her in Rosenthal's words 'the most dismissible of the great modernists'.

(Giles) Lytton Strachey (1880-1932) was an unhappy, sickly child from a large and distinguished family, who finally came into his own at Cambridge and through Virginia Woolf's Bloomsbury gatherings, which brought him the valuable patronage of Ottoline Morrell and the companionship of the painter Dora Carrington, with whom he lived, on and off, in a ménage à trois with her husband, Ralph Partridge. Graded C4 medically and a conspicuous conscien-

194. Giles Lytton Strachey by Max Beerbohm

195. Roger Fry

tious objector to boot, Strachey passed the Great War writing an iconoclastic volume of biographical sketches ironically entitled *Eminent Victorians*; it made his reputation.

None of the other Bloomsbury literati approach Woolf and Strachey in stature or significance. Raymond Mortimer and Desmond MacCarthy (whose wife coined the term 'Bloomsberries') both wrote for the *New Statesman* and the *Sunday Times* and were influential critics, and Robert Trevelyan was a prolific poet. E.M. Forster, T.S. Eliot, Aldous Huxley and Arthur Waley were all well known to the Bloomsbury writers but are more often regarded as having been *among* them than *of* them.

THE ARTISTS

Roger Fry (1866-1934) trained under Sickert but was much more important as an art historian and critic than as an artist. In 1910, with the enthusiastic help of Clive Bell and Desmond MacCarthy, he organised an exhibition - *Manet and the Post-Impressionists* - which introduced the British public to the work of Cézanne, Van Gogh, Gauguin and Matisse. The general reaction was, to put it mildly, hostile (the use of 'Bloomsbury' as a pejorative term was first coined in respect of the canvases on display at the Grafton Gallery), but the exhibition had a formative impact on the Bloomsbury painters, Vanessa Bell and Duncan Grant. Fry summarised his own aesthetic theories, emphasising the significance of form over subject-matter, in *Vision and Design* (1920). Alan and Veronica Palmer hit the mark nicely in summarising its objective:

' If Roger Fry was Bloomsbury's Ruskin, he declined to function as an interpreter of artistic content; he preferred.... to teach the perception of painting, as if it were music touching the eyes.'

Fry's lovers included Ottoline Morrell, the bohemian model and painter Nina Hamnett, Vanessa Bell and the suffragette Philippa Strachey; he finally settled down at 48 Bernard Street with Helen, estranged wife of the mosaicist Boris Anrep, who included many Bloomsbury figures in his mosaic floor for the National Gallery vestibule.

Duncan Grant (1885-1978) was a relative of the Strachey family and a school-friend of Rupert Brooke. In his youth he rejected Lytton Strachey's advances but accepted those of J.M. Keynes, with whom he shared rooms in Fitzroy Square, before moving into 38 Brunswick Square. A friend of Matisse and Picasso, he enjoyed the patronage of Roger Fry with whom he established the avant-garde Omega workshops at 33 Fitzroy Square - where Nina Hamnett did most of the work. High-spirited, good-humoured and charming, he also partnered the ballerina Lydia Lopokova (Keynes's wife) in ballet-skits at parties but was attracted to both Vanessa Bell and the writer David Garnett - who eventually married Angelica, the daughter born to Vanessa as a result of a brief affair with Duncan. He continued to advise Keynes on his art purchses and enjoyed in return his generous financial support.

Art critic David Piper's verdict on the collection of Bloomsbury art that Roger Fry bequeathed to the Courtauld gallery was that they were: '.... a little sad and a little drab; paintings of painstaking honesty, yet lacking that final ruthlessness that kindles painting into greatness.'

IN SUMMARY

In an irritable memoir Clive Bell noted that the term 'Bloomsbury' had been variously used as though it implied 'a point of view, a period, a gang of conspirators or an infectious disease.' Denying the existence of any specific credo and emphasising the extent to which the dozen or so 'core members' of the alleged Group actually criticised each other's works and opinions, he averred in conclusion that 'beyond mutual liking they had precious little in common.' The *Encyclopaedia Britannica* endorses this view but is generous in its estimation of the Group's influence: '... the Bloomsbury group did not constitute a school. Its significance lies in the extraordinary number of talented persons associated with it.'

(Other personalities close enough to the Group to merit entries in *Who's Who in Bloomsbury* include the artists Leon Bakst, Andre Derain, Gerald Kelly and Wyndham Lewis and the writers Gerald Brenan, David Cecil, Christopher Isherwood, Vita Sackville-West and Hugh Walpole, not to mention Diaghilev and no less than eleven Stracheys.)

Michael Rosenthal, no unbiased observer admittedly, argues forcefully that a positive re-evaluation of the Bloomsbury phenomenon has occurred in recent years: '... what was once seen as trivial and pernicious is instead hailed as prophetic and socially redemptive.... For a culture that is.... trying to divest itself of the rigidities of traditional sexual role-playing.... the value the Bloomsberries are seen to place on friendship and art, and their rejection of the use of power in personal relationships, bring them into the cultural mainstream from which they were so long excluded.'

Destruction and Development

'IMPROVEMENTS'

Bloomsbury was largely built up, and its 'character' established, by the 1830s - just in time for that character to be challenged by two powerful forces which were to change the face of the entire capital - the advent of the railways and the emergence of more active and effective forms of metropolitan government and charitable action. Railways made it possible for existing Bloomsbury residents to decamp to new commuter suburbs, vacating homes which could provide short-term accommodation for students, scholars and tourists taking advantage of easier access to the area's facilities. The reform movement led to piecemeal schemes for 'improvement', involving slum clearance, the construction of 'model dwellings' and the provision of public facilities, as varied as libraries, wash-houses and drill-halls for 'Saturday night soldiers'. The completion of New Oxford Street in 1847 represented quite literally a major breakthrough in clearing the notorious slum area which lay to the south of Great Russell Street.

TRANSPORTS OF DELIGHT?

Improvements in London's transport system - railways, better roads, omnibuses - led many of Bloomsbury's better-off residents to give up keeping their own carriages and use either public facilities or a hired hansom or hackney as the occasion demanded. The mews courtyards originally built for private carriage accommodation often became livery-stables, packed with hacks for the hire-trade, and thus breeding-grounds for flies and germs. The demolition of these black-spots (eg in the areas behind Torrington Square and Keppel Street), between the 1880s and the Great War, was regarded by local residents as a major environmental improvement.

At the very same time that the mews nuisance was being dispelled another emerged to replace it. In 1890 the newly-established London County Council secured from Parliament the London Streets (Removal of Gates) Act. Against much local opposition the LCC used its new powers to require the dismantling of fifteen barriers, erected under the terms of an Act of 1800, which had enabled the Bedford estate to secure its inhabitants against the nuisance of through-traffic. Between 1891 and 1893 they all came down.

Traffic was further intensified by the construction of the Northern and Piccadilly Underground lines in the 1890s and of Kingsway, complete with tram-tunnel, in the first decade of the new century.

196. Two drill halls were built in the Bloomsbury area, one in Chenies Street, the other, seen below, in Duke's Road by St Pancras church. Both are now auditoriums. Chenies Street is a mixed-arts establishment and Duke's Road is the headquarters of The Place, one of London's premier modern dance venues. Depicted is the opening in 1889 of the headquarters of the Twentieth Middlesex (Artists') Rifles, by the Prince of Wales.

197. *The Gower Street gate bar, which was abolished in April 1893, stood as shown just to the north of the entrance to University College.*

198. *The gate across Gordon Street, abolished in 1893.*

199. *The Kingsway tram tunnel.*

'MODEL DWELLINGS'

The construction of major new thoroughfares and the building of railways necessarily involved large-scale slum-clearance. But as there was no obligation on the promoters of these schemes to rehouse those displaced they were simply dispersed to other slums where the crowding consequently became even worse. A more positive response to their needs was represented by the movement to provide 'model dwellings'. To the modern eye these often seem bleak, barrack-like and oppressive. This impression is not entirely misleading. Model dwellings required model tenants. They were carefully selected and subjected to close surveillance; there was no room for the shiftless, much less the criminal. Professor Olsen hits the mark squarely in describing these mini-estates as 'training schools for the inculcation of middle-class virtues among the lower, but aspiring, orders.'

Despite their forbidding appearance, blocks of model apartments represented a huge advance on what they replaced. They were solidly built, well-ventilated and provided with proper water and sewerage arrangements. Many were built around paved, enclosed areas, where children could play, safe and supervised.

200. *The Streatham Street Model Buildings, as depicted in* The Builder *in July 1849.*

Bloomsbury still boasts one of the earliest examples of this novel architectural genre, the Model Dwellings for Families, erected in Streatham Street to the designs of Henry Roberts in 1849, for the Society for Improving the Condition of the Labouring Classes. The site was provided by the Duke of Bedford for a nominal ground-rent. Roberts went on to become something of a specialist in this field, advising Prince Albert on community architecture a century before the present Prince of Wales acquired a similar con

201. *The slums of Keppel Mews, between Torrington Place and Montague Place, were displaced when Malet Street was constructed.*

202. *St Pancras Mission House in Sandwich Street.*

No. 104. August, 1863. Price One Penny. | THE BRITISH WORKMAN. | Registered for Transmission Abroad.

203. *Preparing for the flower show at St George's Bloomsbury. From* The British Workman, *August 1863.*

cern. Featuring open-access galleries, nowadays gaily bedecked with window-boxes, the Streatham Street dwellings are ranged around a courtyard and have been warmly, if ambiguously, praised by Pevsner as 'surprisingly dignified, as compared with later Peabody horrors'.

The Peabody horrors referred to are the legacy of George Peabody (1795-1869), an American banker-philanthropist whose bequest of £500,000 was used to rehouse thousands of the capital's 'respectable' poor. Bloomsbury's share of this bounty can be seen at the northern end of Herbrand Street, where four courts of slum houses were demolished in 1884 to make way for eight blocks of tenements with 420 rooms.

Later examples of Victorian model blocks can be found between Regent Square and Argyle Square, built in the 1890s and 1900s by the East End Dwellings Company Ltd. and by St Pancras Borough Council - significantly under the auspices of the Public Health Committee.

GOING DOWN?

Despite the manifest 'improvements' of Victoria's reign contemporaries tended to see Bloomsbury as an area which had already declined from fashionable elegance to mere respectability and was now in danger of sliding into a shabby gentility that was more shabby than genteel.

Some parts of Bloomsbury, especially to the north and east of the Bedford estate, had inhabitants who were very poor indeed. Newspapers of the 1840s and 1850s reported court proceedings relating to robberies at brothels and illegal prize-fights for cash prizes in this area.

The comfortable classes sensed potential danger and supported initiatives to relieve distress and provide moral uplift, wholesome diversion and self-improvement. A soup kitchen established in Sandwich Street in 1848 dispensed 48,000 meals over the following two years - plus forty-eight pints of port. An infants' school, the second in the area, was subsequently established over its premises. The St Pancras Mission House built in Sandwich Street in 1873 combined a chapel for two hundred with a playground and a large 'needlework room'.

By the 1860s the Flower Show held annually in Russell Square attracted some four hundred local entrants, mostly from among the poor. Contemporary press coverage emphasised the importance of the occasion in promoting polite contact across class-barriers. In 1864 the prizes were presented by that embodiment of patrician reformers, Lord Shaftesbury himself. He not only gave rosettes and ribbons for blooms and blossoms but also distributed cash rewards of up to £2 to tenants judged by the local Rector to have kept their rooms most neat and tidy.

(The dutiful clergyman inspected no less than six hundred in the course of selecting his nominees.)

Too much should not be made of allegations of social decline. Even if the streets had largely fallen to the invincible onslaught of the landladies by the turn of the century, the squares still boasted residents who were not only well-to-do but socially prominent as well. Russell Square was home to Sir Edward Clarke, a barrister so successful that he virtually halved his annual income by accepting 'promotion' to the post of Solicitor General.   Ex-Prime Minister Asquith

204. *The massive Liverpool Victoria office block which fronts Southampton Row and intrudes upon the harmony of Bloomsbury Square.*

205. *As offices and commerce centred on Holborn so there was a need to teach office skills. Pitman's (shown below) established its main teaching school in Southampton Row.*

206. *The large number of single people drawn to central London by the lure of employment inspired the rapid development of hostels for men and women. Above is the YMCA headquarters in Tottenham Court Road, as depicted in* The Building News, *13 August, 1902, a building now replaced by a modern block.*

207. *Sicilian Avenue, a stylish addition to Southampton Row.*

208. *Herbert Henry Asquith.*

moved into Bedford Square after resigning himself to the permanence of his resignation - at least until Lady Asquith, a formidable rival to Ottoline Morrell in the hostess stakes, decided that the house was too small for entertaining on a satisfactory scale.

CAMPUS CONFUSIONS

In 1910 a Royal Commission on University Education in London was appointed under the chairmanship of Lord Haldane. At that time the University of London's main administration and library were unsatisfactorily housed within the confines of the Imperial Institute at South Kensington. One of the Haldane Commission's main recommendations therefore was that:

'The university should have for its headquarters permanent buildings appropriate in design to its dignity and importance, adequate in extent and specially constructed for its purposes, situated conveniently for the work it has to do, bearing its name and under its own control.'

Mews clearance north of the British Museum had created a large open space ripe for re-development but, despite University interest in it, nothing definite was done beyond the submission of grandiose archi-

209. *An aerial view of Senate House and surrounding University buildings.*

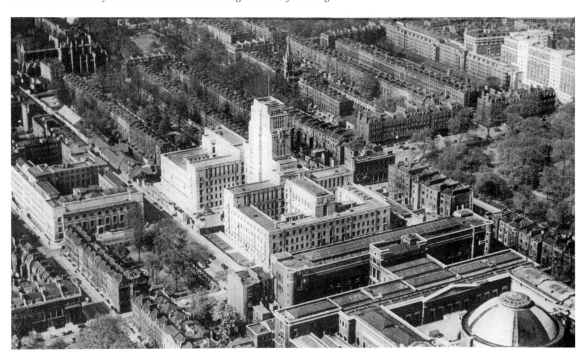

tectural sketches by Lutyens and other eminent architects who sniffed a major commission. During the Great War part of this site served as allotments (tilled by the men of Tottenham Court Road police station), while the 'Shakespeare Hut' served as a club and canteen for servicemen where the London School of Hygiene and Tropical Medicine now stands.

University interest in the Bloomsbury site revived in 1920 and it was purchased by the government from the Duke of Bedford to provide a home not only for an administration block and library but also for King's College, which would vacate its Strand site. 'Shakespeare Hut' became a club for Indian students. In 1921 the Institute of Historical Research moved into a temporary home on Malet Street which resembled a cross between a Tudor manor house and an elongated cricket pavilion. This building was initially shared with the newly-established Institute of International Affairs (which moved over to Chatham House in St. James's Square in 1924) and then with the School of Slavonic Studies. Little more was done, however, to advance the main scheme and King's withdrew its interest. Plans to turn 'Shakespeare Hut' into a National Theatre collapsed and the site was bought by the Rockefeller Foundation, which gave it to the School of Hygiene and Tropical Medicine, whose new building was opened by Health Minister Neville Chamberlain in 1930. In 1922 the first head-quarters office of the National Union of Students was established in Endsleigh Street, beginning an association with the Bloomsbury area that has lasted until the present time.

In 1926 the government suddenly sold the proposed university precinct back to the Duke of Bedford. This prompted a dramatic initiative by the Vice-Chancellor, Sir William Beveridge, who visited America and returned triumphant with a Rockefeller cheque for £400,000. When topped up with a government grant this transatlantic munificence finally enabled the University to secure the land outright for £525,000. It was subsequently decided that, apart from its existing occupants, the area should also provide a home for the Courtauld Institute of Art, the Institute of Education, the School of Oriental Studies and Birkbeck College.

London House, a residential centre in Mecklenburgh Square for overseas students, was opened in 1930, built to the designs of Sir Herbert Baker - an appropriate choice in the light of his major project, New Delhi, the capital of British India.

The foundation stone of the projected university centre was laid by George V in 1933 and the first phase of Charles Holden's monumental Senate House occupied in 1936, the centenary year of the University's charter.

210. A drawing of the new Senate House buildings, as featured on a contemporary postcard.

In the Shadow of the Senate

BLOOMSBURY AT WAR

War-time Bloomsbury had much of the air of a transit camp as whole categories of strangers made it their temporary domicile before moving on to safety or even greater danger elsewhere. Soon after the outbreak of hostilities hundreds of civilian refugees from Gibraltar were billeted in the hotels along Great Russell Street. The former Palace Hotel on Bloomsbury Street housed the offices of relief organisations which did what they could to sustain and relocate exiles from occupied Europe and, later, orphan children from the concentration camps. Canadian troops occupied many of the hotels on the northern side of Bloomsbury, while Warwickshire House on Gower Street became a club for all the services to use. From the Byng Place headquarters of the Women's Farm and Garden Association the Women's Land Army was organised and directed. Meanwhile, discreetly, in an underground bunker beneath Alfred Place staff-officers planned the Allied invasion of Europe. (The appropriately-named Eisenhower Centre is now a security archive for documentation.)

Towering over the whole area, metaphorically as well as literally, was the recently completed University Senate House which was occupied by the Ministry of Information and most of its notorious 999 employees. Writers, broadcasters, journalists and film-makers haunted its corridors and committee-rooms, seeking permissions, clearances and access to people, places and resources. Some of the most eminent took their literary revenge in due course. Holden's forbidding Portland stone tower provided Orwell with the model for the Ministry of Truth in *1984*. For Graham Greene it became the *Ministry of Fear*. Evelyn Waugh used it as the setting for an hilarious episode in *Put Out More Flags,* in which a lunatic with a bomb in a briefcase is blithely referred from one department to another, clutching his ticking burden all the while.

211. *The bombing of Bloomsbury Dispensary.*

212. *A fund-raising parade in Holborn. The front section of the march are Civil Defence members.*

Elsewhere in Bloomsbury other literary figures were 'doing their bit', as the saying went. In the Russell Square offices of Faber & Faber T.S. Eliot took his turn at fire-watching on Tuesday nights until the premises were bombed out. In Lansdowne Terrace Orwell's ex-Etonian school chum, the hedonistic Cyril Connolly was, somehow, managing to produce *Horizon*, an avant-garde arts magazine which won a cult following among the more intellectual servicemen, who saw in it an exemplar of the values they were fighting to defend. Connolly's collaborator, the poet Stephen Spender, not only assisted in the noble cause but served as an auxiliary fireman as well. Poet John Lehmann (another old Etonian) acted as general manager of the Hogarth Press and edited the influential volumes of Penguin New Writing as well.

According to Lehmann's subsequent history of Holborn Bloomsbury was a dangerous place to be. Over a seventh of the buildings in the borough of Holborn were destroyed and 426 people killed; in proportion to the area involved this was worse than

anywhere else in the capital and, indeed, the kingdom. The Bloomsbury Dispensary and the Hogarth Press were destroyed outright. RADA and St. Peter's, Regent Square suffered direct hits. So did the West Central Synagogue and Jewish Girls' Club in Alfred Place; twenty-seven people sheltering in the basement were killed outright. Damage to buildings was especially severe right along the northern side of Theobald's Road.

RECONSTRUCTION OR RAPE?

Writing around 1950 Pevsner was inclined to commend the slab-like blocks of flats hastily thrown up in Dombey Street and Cromer Street: '.... although they do not make a symmetrical composition, the informal way in which they range themselves and the lawns between them make them highly impressive.'

The buildings that have followed since then - such as the TUC headquarters in Great Russell Street (1958), uncompromising Brunswick Centre (1972), the new YMCA on Great Russell Street (1976), the

213. *More serious than damage caused by bombing was the state of the fabric of houses in many parts of Bloomsbury, caused either by long neglect, the war, or a combination of both. Terraces were so dilapidated that they were thought to be beyond repair and, in any case, a waste of money compared with new dwellings. The Bedford Estate conserved and updated most of its property but in other areas there was demolition. However, the terraces which make up Woburn Walk were saved. These are shown above and overleaf as they were in 1922.*

214. *Woburn Buildings (Walk) in 1922.*

215. *Much conservation was carried out by private indivuduals moving into the northern part of Bloomsbury. Regent Square, despite the loss of its two churches, was gradually restored. Pictured to the right is a drawing of No. 3 Regent Square.*

216. *A derelict terrace in Brunswick Square, 1953.*

217. *The Brunswick Centre on the Foundling Estate.*

218. *The TUC Building, Great Russell Street.*

student hostels on Cartwright Gardens, the office-blocks, police station and library on Theobald's Road - may arguably have been 'better built' but have won far less praise.

Writing in 1966 architectural critic Ian Nairn observed bitterly: 'As anything more than an area on a map, Bloomsbury is dead. Town planners and London University have killed it between them - a notable academic victory. The splendid plane trees are still there to soothe... But instead of their gay yet discreet stock-brick surroundings, there are doughy intrusions like the droppings of an elephant. The original was built.... to make a profit and be an enjoyable part of London as well. The replacements are designed from God knows what backwater of the intellect. If this is progress, then I am a total abstainer.'

In a history of Holborn published in 1970 ex-Bloomsbury John Lehmann predicted querulously: '.... it seems likely that it will not be many decades before Burton's Bloomsbury is found to have disappeared except for a few isolated rows, or remnants of rows, to remind us of man-sized architecture in a vanished age of taste.... a huge area between Coram Street and Bernard Street has been razed to make way for tourist hotels and London University is about to gobble up Woburn Square.'

London University did, indeed, gobble up Woburn Square, demolishing Vulliamy's Christ Church to make way for Sir Denys Lasdun's Institute of Education building and extension to the School of Oriental and African Studies. A plan to raze the area immediately south of the British Museum, so as to build a new British Library was, however, aborted.

However much the physical fabric of Bloomsbury may have changed its essential character has endured. When the Borough of Holborn was created in 1901 it adopted as its motto *Multi pertransibunt et Augebiter Scientia*. Even though the Borough itself was abolished in 1965, when Bloomsbury was absorbed into Camden, the meaning of the motto remains entirely appropriate - 'Many shall pass through and knowledge will be increased.'

INDEX

(Asterisks indicate pages on
which illustrations
appear)